Annual Giving

A Practical Approach

Fritz W. Schroeder

CASE Books

ISBN 0-89964-357-4
Printed in the United States of America

Council for Advancement and Support of Education (CASE) is an international education association, serving professionals in the disciplines of alumni relations, communications, and philanthropy.

CASE offers high-quality training, information resources, and a wide variety of books, videotapes, and materials for advancement professionals.

Visit our CASE Books online catalog at *www.case.org/books.*
To receive our printed catalog, call (202) 328-2273.

Book design: Fletcher Design
Editors: Robin Netherton and Andrea Hill

CASE Books

COUNCIL FOR ADVANCEMENT
AND SUPPORT OF EDUCATION
1307 New York Avenue, NW
Suite 1000
Washington, DC 20005-4701

This book is dedicated to my father, Frederic W. Schroeder Jr. Each of us, whether in university advancement or elsewhere, should aspire to a career that would parallel his—full of honesty, personal integrity, compassion, unselfish service, and a love for the spirit of education.

Contents

Foreword

Not long ago, annual giving programs had the run of the philanthropic house. Starting in the 1890s and extending for a period of 60 years, annual giving programs in the United States built their logic and established their rhythms without much challenge from other types of fund raising. Individuals were still leaving gifts to their favorite charities via wills, of course, but the stock and trade of the philanthropy business was annual giving.

During this period, large-scale capital campaigns were occasionally conducted, but were seen as arising from crisis: our dining hall has been destroyed by fire; we must rebuild! The notion that campaigns could be justified by how education was financed—i.e. the gap between tuition (price) and expense (cost)—and not by crisis alone, was not really understood, much less accepted. With the GIs returning from World War II and the ranks of colleges and universities swelling beyond reasonable capacity, the need for larger and repeated infusions of money became vital. Annual giving programs could not provide these resources, but capital campaigns could, so they were embraced and moved to center stage.

As the modern capital campaign emerged, the bequest and estate programs also gained in prominence. Some instigating factors for the rise of these programs may have been the perception of continuous changes in individual tax rates, especially concerning gift and estate laws; as well as ever-escalating levels of wealth and the need to preserve and pass it on. Whatever the cause, it soon became clear to many future philanthropists that the trust program, and not an outright gift or a gift via a bequest, was the way to go. Like the large-scale campaign, today's bequest and trust programs—now known as planned giving—have developed their own identity. And annual giving? In some quarters, this program was being seen as an out-dated method of raising funds.

Under these circumstances, it is wonderful and even surprising to see someone like Fritz Schroeder, a self-described "Generation X-er," advocate annual giving. What is so refreshing about this book is not that Fritz has tried to reinvent the annual giving wheel, but that instead has had the forthrightness and wisdom to see that this tried and tested form of fund raising can speak to today's new generation of donors. I watched him develop this approach during our years together at the CASE Summer Institute in Educational Fund Raising. Looking to replace a fabulous set of teachers in the annual giving track, I turned to Fritz hoping that he would use this session to present his ideas on annual giving and demonstrate practices that he had already field-tested. The insight and originality of Fritz's first course was startling. Annual giving suddenly became more exciting, more entrepreneurial. Over the next two years, he refined his approach and has now used it as the basis for this wonderful book.

Consider, for example, his use of "Real-Life Points for Practice" in this book. These sections add new and practical exercises to what might otherwise be considered a traditionally theoretical approach to annual giving. These exercises help the reader transfer and apply the basics of annual giving into his or her own world. Fritz has not only offered some of the best thinking in this field, but he has asked the reader to contribute his or her own thoughts and experiences into the equation.

Yes, annual giving is the grandfather of all organized philanthropy. In this book, Fritz has not simply presented the workings of annual giving, he has brought it to life.

Paul E. Sheff
Vice President, Development and Alumni Relations
College of the Holy Cross

Preface

Recently, a colleague asked me about the goal of this book: "Is it a 'how-to' book or a theory book?" The best way for me to answer that question is to jump to the end. When you finish this book, if you are new to the field, you will have a thorough overview of both the theory and the practice of annual giving. You will understand the principles of organizing, implementing, and evaluating an annual giving program. Furthermore, you will grasp the relationships between annual giving and overall development efforts, campaigns, alumni relations, and your institution. If you have already been in annual giving for a while, you will, I hope, have many of your instincts reaffirmed or even expanded. Most important though, is that you should find a few new ideas or new ways of looking at the familiar.

The next logical question, then, is "How will we accomplish this?" First, the book is organized into four sections. It begins with a discussion of annual giving theory: what the annual fund is, how you organize it, and its role in your institution. These are the issues that should constantly be playing in the background as you manage an annual giving program. The next two sections address the day-to-day activities of annual giving: the tools, solicitation techniques, programs, and events that drive annual giving efforts every year. The final section walks through planning and evaluation so that you can combine the theory of annual giving with the day-to-day activities and organize a well-developed, comprehensive program.

Second, throughout the book, you will find a series of exercises titled "Real-Life Points for Practice." By undertaking these exercises as you read, you should finish the book with a clear set of strategies you can implement immediately or explore as you choose. You will not find anything in these "Real-Life Points" that spells out how to write a phonathon script, how to start a parents program, or how to convert a nondonor to a donor in five fast steps. You won't find these because it's never that simple and because every institution is unique.

You will find, however, that the "Real-Life Points" offer steps and questions that will help you focus your time and energy more efficiently to improve your program. These exercises will show you how to differentiate between the symptoms of a problem and the problem itself, and how to determine which causes you can influence and which you cannot. Your responsibility (or the responsibility of the person whom you choose to delegate it to) is to use these points to help you identify the strengths and shortcomings of your program, and make careful, determined decisions about what you can eliminate, reinforce, or improve.

Finally, I hope this book will help you understand the wonderful complexity of what you do in development and, more specifically, in annual giving. This work is both creative and quantitative, a mix that requires you to think in the long term but act in the short term. It requires an understanding of individuals as well as the masses, and to do it well, you must blend marketing with personal selling strategies.

As we continue, you will notice the repeated use of the terms "institution," "president/CEO," "constituents," and other references that reflect the fact that the ideas in this book have been developed within the higher education environment. However, while there will certainly be sections that are relevant only in education (senior class gift strategies, for example), this book will be helpful for anyone exploring the annual giving arena. If you are involved in annual giving for a social services agency, a religious organization, an arts association, or another type of nonprofit organization, I am sure you can adapt some of these concepts to your environment. I wish you success in your efforts.

Acknowledgments

First, I need to offer thanks and appreciation to the three peer reviewers who gave their time to read the truly "rough" draft of this book. Their insight, opinions, suggestions, and encouragement have been invaluable: Courtney Dunakin, director of annual giving, Children's Memorial Foundation of Chicago; Karin George, vice president for development and alumnae relations, Smith College; and Joseph Kender, assistant vice president for development and alumni relations, Georgetown University.

I need to acknowledge the encouragement and support of Nancy Raley, Norma Walker, and their colleagues in CASE Books.

Thanks also to JoAnne Surette for her editorial advice.

Additionally, I have had the opportunity to work for a very talented set of professionals throughout the last 12 years, including Ed Kardos at James Madison University; Kathryn Costello, Bill Lynerd, and Leonard Raley at the University of Maryland; and Jan Corazza, Mary Blair, and Bob Lindgren at Johns Hopkins University. They will each recognize their influences in sections of this book.

Finally, I am truly fortunate to not only have a rewarding work life, but to also have the gift of family that makes me race home every evening: Amy, Maddie, and Eric, with my love.

Introduction

Annual giving is the genesis of all development. Before there were campaigns, million-dollar donors, and sophisticated tracking systems, there was the annual fund campaign. Early Greek philosophers spoke of the importance of sustaining society's vital institutions through regular financial commitments. Many religious institutions have promoted regular tithing since their founding. Organizations such as the YMCA and Salvation Army have sought annual contributions using mail campaigns and volunteer solicitors for more than a century.

Today, in our comprehensive development programs, the annual fund is still the cornerstone of our fund-raising efforts. In the simplest sense, raising money for the annual fund is all about acquiring, retaining, and upgrading donors. It operates on an annual cycle, hence the term "annual fund." Every year, the program starts over at square one. The process involves efforts that convince last year's donors to renew their support, while simultaneously developing a case that encourages nondonors to join the ranks for the first time. The effort to retain last year's donors relies heavily on the "habit-forming" aspect of making annual gifts, but also demands that consistent messages of stewardship and donor accountability be sent throughout the year. Acquiring new donors is a more expensive effort that involves regular, repeated solicitations with a clear, compelling case for support.

The annual fund plays many different roles in the institution. To the development program, the annual fund is

- the public face of fund raising,
- a source of potential major gift donors,
- a vehicle for communication, and
- a way to involve constituents.

To the institution, the annual fund is

- an important source of revenue, and
- a connection with alumni and other valued constituents.

To donors, the annual fund is

- a way to invest in an institution,
- a way to indicate support for an institution,
- the only communication with the institution they may have in any given year, and
- a tradition.

One of the most challenging aspects of managing or planning an annual giving program is to answer the popular question "What do you count in your annual fund?" With major gifts, corporate and foundation gifts, and planned gifts, the criteria for "counting" a gift are fairly straightforward (and in the case of planned giving, definitions are carefully directed by the Internal Revenue Service, planned giving advisory groups, and other organizations). By contrast, the method we use to define annual gifts often differs dramatically from one institution to the next. Many programs only count truly unrestricted gifts in their annual fund totals, while others may include all current-use gifts (gifts that are to be spent within a short time period). Another program may look at all giving under a certain dollar threshold (say, $1,000 or $10,000), and still others may use one single account as their annual fund.

Although there isn't a single definition of "the annual fund" at work in our institutions, there are several general guidelines:

- Annual gifts should be for current-use purposes (to be spent this year).
- In an ideal world, annual gifts should be unrestricted.
- The size of the annual gift is not terribly relevant.

Let's examine each of these statements in greater detail.

Annual gifts should be for current use. One of the ways we promote the annual fund is to identify the impact annual gifts have on the day-to-day life of our institutions. While gifts to our endowments secure the institutional future, gifts to the annual fund help provide for the "excellence of today." Therefore, annual fund gifts are made with assets that are immediately expendable, and to an account or fund that is for current-use purposes such as operating expenses, scholarships, or outreach programs.

Annual gifts should be unrestricted. This guideline really does vary with every program. Unrestricted gifts provide the leadership of our institutions with the greatest flexibility to address immediate needs and opportunities. However, unrestricted annual giving presupposes trust in the administration (CEO, trustees, etc.), which will be "spending" annual gifts. This makes unrestricted dollars among the most challenging to raise—and perhaps the most rewarding. Conversely, there are hundreds of very successful programs that do not place a strong emphasis on unrestricted giving, instead allowing donors to designate gifts everywhere from architecture to zoology. As you can imagine, the decision to emphasize unrestricted giving or designated giving is a balance between the need for unrestricted revenue and donor interests.

The size of the gift is not really relevant. More specifically, the size of the gift is not really relevant to defining the "annual fund." Our programs receive gifts ranging from $1 to $1 million. They all count. However, the size of the gift is important to the donor. For us to include a gift in the annual fund, the assumption is that the gift should be repeatable again in subsequent years and, therefore, annually. If we were to include a $50,000 gift in our annual fund figures for this year, knowing that the donor does not have the capacity or the inclination to repeat that gift next year, two things are inevitable: (1) we significantly raise the expectations for next year's fund without the ability to repeat that performance, and (2) we fail to create an awareness of the importance of annual support from this donor in a way that might lead to a gift the following year. There are exceptions, of course, such as one-time gifts made in honor or memory of someone, but the inclusion of nonrepeatable gifts in the annual fund undermines the very premise of annual giving.

Before we move on to a specific discussion of the theory and practice of the annual fund, let's review a few important concepts that provide a context for the ideas in this book.

To begin with, the words "annual giving" and "annual fund" are almost interchangeable, yet they can be confusing to newcomers. For the purposes of our discussion, we'll interpret them as follows:

"Annual giving" refers to a process. We work on annual giving programs; we develop annual giving strategies; perhaps we are staff members within an office of annual giving. "Annual giving" also refers to all facets of the program—direct mail, reunions, parents, gift societies, etc.

"Annual fund" refers to the dollars that are raised toward the established goal. We may say that XYZ's annual fund was $100,000 in the last fiscal year. The term "annual fund" may also refer to a single account in institutions whose culture promotes purely unrestricted annual gifts.

Other interchangeable terms are associated with telephone and direct mail fund-raising programs. We refer to "telemarketing," "phonathons," "telethons," and "call-a-thons" to describe the types of programs that use the telephone and a paid or volunteer caller to solicit gifts from individuals. In the same manner, we use terms such as "direct mail," "mail appeals," and "mail solicitations" to solicit gifts from individuals through the mail.

Annual giving efforts can also be complicated by the way we determine our yearly schedule. To our donors, the calendar year is really the only significant timeline. However, our institutions may operate on a fiscal year that is different from the calendar year. To further complicate the issue, some institutions operate on a fiscal year while maintaining another, separate, fund-raising year. Although rare, these cases do present an unusual set of challenges for planning, projections, and revenue flow. It is crucial that we recognize that the concept of a "year" may be something different for us than it is for our donors, and we need to be sensitive to those differences.

At the end of this book, you will find a list of useful terms that will help you as you learn about the different aspects of annual giving.

SECTION I

The Annual Fund in Theory

The theory of annual giving is not about individual solicitations or statistics, but rather about how the annual fund is positioned within the overall context of your development program and your institution. There is no "right" way of positioning an annual fund, because every institution has characteristics that determine the annual fund's role and relationships.

As you read the chapters in this section, please consider these overriding concepts:

- Annual giving needs definition. If you haven't defined your efforts, you don't know what you're working toward. This definition includes not only what you do, but also why you do it (your goals), and how you measure what you do and its relevance in the overall development effort.
- Annual giving needs context within your organization. If your institution (you, your leadership, your constituency) cannot complete the sentence "The annual fund at our institution is _____," then you need to help provide that context.
- Growing an annual fund is not a job that can be done in a vacuum. It involves partnerships throughout the institution. In this section, we will look at what forms those partnerships may take and how you might approach building them.

The Role of Annual Giving in the Development Program

IN THE INTRODUCTION, WE NOTED THAT DIFFERENT INSTITUTIONS define annual giving by which gifts they choose to count toward the annual fund. There are also other ways in which the role of the annual giving program can vary from one institution to another.

For example, some programs are steeped in tradition with strong alumni participation (50 to 75 percent), outstanding reunion efforts, and a steady stream of current revenue that is an integral part of the institution's financial health. Here, the institution typically views the annual fund as a significant revenue source with the expectation that the broad base of participation will ensure a dependable income. The efforts in this program focus on preserving and growing the base.

In other cases, while the annual fund's contribution to the revenue stream remains important, the institution may view the annual giving program primarily as a feeder to the major gifts effort. Many institutions have determined that, among their alumni, the annual gift has been the single most important predictor for major gift potential, so solicitors visit almost every donor who makes regular annual gifts over a certain threshold—say, $100. In this type of program, development efforts focus on carefully tracking the higher-end donors for consecutive giving and increased giving, and on creating initiatives to increase this pool of major gift prospects.

These are just two examples of the role of annual giving efforts. The crucial issue is that each program clearly understands the role of its institution's annual fund and takes determined action toward specific goals.

Let's explore the possible goals and roles of an annual giving program.

Participation. Although we all want broad-based participation, very few of us can actually claim participation percentages that pass the 50 percent mark. As in baseball, a batting average in the .300s is considered great. Those of us with participation rates in the 30 to 40 percent range should feel good (even though we're not likely to get a three-year, $6 million contract or a place in the Hall of Fame). Overall participation, whether from alumni, parents, friends, or others, is a solid indicator of how our closest friends feel about supporting the institution. That endorsement carries weight with major donors, corporations and foundations, our own faculty and staff, and other observers. In addition, broad participation provides a cushion of support. In today's record economy, we feel great because many donors are giving at levels exceeding our expectations on an annual basis. However, when the market slows and some of these individual donors decrease the size of their gifts, it is the broad base of support that will help sustain the revenue stream.

As a rule of thumb, pursuing broad participation is an expensive proposition. (This is not meant as a negative statement.) Each institution has a "base line" participation rate, the rate that can be achieved through the standard solicitation schedule. For example, if your program typically solicits alumni four times each year—say, with two phone contacts and two mail contacts—and you generally maintain a 28 percent participation rate, then that is your base line. Each year, you add alumni to the roster, and any subtle enhancements that may occur in your program might only enable you to keep pace with the growing alumni list. It will take a significant investment to raise your participation rate in any substantial manner. You might need to double the number of solicitations, increase your alumni relations efforts, add staff, or take some other significant step to achieve your goal.

Major gift cultivation. Every annual giving program can serve as a cultivation and identification tool for major gift efforts. Many of the screening programs offered by national consulting firms point to consecutive annual gift patterns as the single greatest predictor of major gift success. Furthermore, many donors "self-identify" through their gifts to the annual fund. For example, donors who increase their gift from $500 to $2,500 in one year are sending a signal about either their commitment to your organization or their personal financial situation. Finally, annual gifts are an important stewardship step for major donors. Asking major donors to invest in the annual fund further strengthens their relationship to the institution. (We'll focus on the relationship between annual gifts and major gifts in Chapter 4.)

Real-Life Points for Practice

Calculate the number of donors you need to add each year just to maintain the same participation rate. Do this by multiplying the size of your graduating class by your current participation percentage. This "new donor" number is also affected by your donor retention rate. For example, if your current participation rate is 20 percent and you graduate a class of 1,000, you need to add 200 new donors this year to maintain 20 percent participation. However, if you had 10,000 donors last year and only retain 75 percent (in other words, 2,500 donors are "lost"), then your actual new donor acquisition target would have to be 2,700 to maintain a 20 percent participation rate.

Volunteer development. Volunteers play a crucial role in annual giving programs. The annual fund provides a wonderful opportunity to introduce volunteers to the philanthropic nature of your organization. Annual giving volunteers are particularly important in overall volunteer management efforts because they can be short-term, entry-level workers. Most of the roles for volunteers in the annual giving program span a fiscal year. While you may renew many of the volunteers year after year, this short term enables you to carefully evaluate individual volunteers and move those with a true commitment forward to longer-term endeavors.

Revenue. While it seems almost too obvious to mention, a primary role of annual giving programs is to generate annual, expendable, and primarily unrestricted revenue. One of the most effective ways to describe the importance of annual fund revenue is to talk about the cash flow it represents in terms of endowment. For example, an annual fund of $200,000 may not appear very significant for some organizations. However, that $200,000 revenue stream represents the equivalent of the income produced by an endowment of $4 million, assuming a 5 percent payout rate.

Real-Life Points for Practice

Calculate the revenue stream and equivalent endowment size of your annual fund. Explore ways to incorporate this message into your materials, solicitations, and presentations.

Creating the Annual Fund Culture at Your Institution

ON PAPER IT IS VERY EASY TO IDENTIFY MANY OF THE FACTORS THAT help or hinder the creation of an annual fund that is rich in tradition, well positioned, and enjoys broad participation. Controlling those factors is a different matter. Let's be honest—there are parts of our institutional culture that we're not going to be able to affect. Our organizations, for the most part, existed for years, decades, or centuries before we arrived, and will continue long beyond our tenure. We have winning sports teams, losing sports teams, or no teams at all. We have histories of rigorous or not-so-rigorous academic programs; too few social activities for students or too many. All of these factors may influence the perceptions of who we are as an institution, and there is little we can do to alter these perceptions.

We can, however, influence our culture in a way that promotes the idea of annual giving and the need for the ongoing involvement of alumni, parents, and friends. At the most basic level, we accomplish this by being vocal and determined advocates for the annual giving program. We should regularly ask, "What message does this send about the importance of ongoing, annual support of our institution?" Or perhaps the question is better phrased, "What does this do to further our constituents' understanding of the irreplaceable nature of their gifts, and to strengthen their enduring commitment to our institution?" In both of these questions, "this" refers to almost any initiative coming from or affecting the development program: printed materials, events, the remarks of the president, the theme of the campaign, thank-you letters, the alumni magazine...and the list goes on and on.

We can prioritize what we do by identifying our areas of influence within our institution. The further we move from our own area, however, the less control we can exert. Still, we can work to cultivate some voice in each of these areas.

The annual giving program. Luckily, the first place to start is typically the one we can best control. If our institution is going to have a culture for annual giving, then the pacesetter for that culture is the program itself. We establish this culture through compelling, consistent messages that reach our constituents on a regular basis. We also strengthen this culture by creating a sense of stewardship for every donor by communicating the importance and the impact of their gifts.

The development program. Beyond the annual giving program, we need to pay attention to what type of climate our overall fund-raising efforts are creating. This, too, is an area that may be within our reach. One of the single greatest challenges any annual giving program faces is how to create a sense of urgency and importance for annual gifts—say, those in the $50 to $500 range—when our overall development efforts are securing six- or even seven-figure, headline-grabbing gifts. The very strongest programs are those successful in creating the relationships that lead to large gifts while also finding a way to make even the most modest donor feel integral to the institution. It's understandable that the $25 donor to the annual fund would be perplexed to receive the same type of recognition and publicity as the largest benefactors. Thus, our strategies with annual and major gift donors should be different, if only because of the size of the philanthropic capability. The challenge lies in creating legitimate, proportional feelings of gratitude, inclusiveness, and partnership that leave all donors confident about their investment. (We'll explore the relationship with other elements of the development program further in Chapters 3, 4, and 5.)

The alumni relations office. Depending on the structure of your institution, the alumni association may be an integral part of your advancement program or a completely separate organization. Regardless of the configuration, the alumni outreach program has a significant impact on your annual fund. It's a truism that the most common negative response from prospective donors is "I only hear from you when you want money." Herein lies the purpose of the alumni association. While the motivations of the programs are different, their objectives are essentially the same: to create stronger relationships between the institution and its constituents. In order to be successful in your annual fund efforts, you must be confident that the alumni program is working hard to create and strengthen those relationships. Establish a partnership with your alumni director even if collaboration between your offices is uncommon. You will both benefit in the long term. (We'll discuss the relationship with the alumni program in more detail in Chapter 3.)

The administration. As we move further from our own program, our ability to influence culture becomes less pronounced. Many of the more prominent spokespersons for our institutions are not members of the development staff. First and foremost, our president, head, or CEO can be the greatest asset to our annual fund strategy, provided our leaders are connected to the culture we're trying to create. For example, when Gerhard Casper arrived at Stanford in the early 1990s, alumni participation hovered around 23 percent. Through several strategic changes to the program, and, more importantly, through the champion efforts of President Casper, alumni participation reached 35 percent during the 1998-99 school year. Chris Ponce, director of the Stanford Fund, refers to the president's remarks as always containing the two pillars—annual giving and endowment. Anytime he spoke before an appropriate audience, the president reflected on the importance of annual, sustaining gifts as well as the need to increase Stanford's endowment. In addition to the president, our vice presidents, provosts, deans, and other senior leaders can also be significant allies of our development efforts and the annual giving program.

Student programs. How many times have you heard the objection, "I would have given if it hadn't been for that parking ticket I got." You can substitute just about anything for parking ticket: an erroneous bill from the bursar, a rejected registration from the scheduling office, a mistaken room assignment from housing, and so forth. The reality is that we are involved in very complex institutions, trying to serve hundreds if not thousands of individuals. Accidents, bungles, mistakes, and oversights do occur. What is true of the registrar's office, the parking authority, and the student housing administration is equally true for every academic department, athletic program, and other curricular or extracurricular activity in which students are involved during their days on campus. Clearly, we cannot control most of these factors, or predict which of them will affect a graduate's later opinion of the institution. However, we do know, both anecdotally and from quantitative attitudinal surveys, that the current alumni perception of our institution can be dramatically influenced by their experience as students. It's not simply a matter of one parking ticket; it's the way we treat students while they are with us that affects their propensity to give in later years.

Let's admit that the concept of influencing a culture that will create graduates who are more likely to give is overwhelming at best. Large service-driven corporations, such as the Walt Disney Companies, Sheraton, and L.L. Bean work 365 days a year to create a culture in which every member, from executive leaders to housekeeping staff, further the idea that the customer is valued and is "wanted back."

So, how do we begin to address this issue in an environment that does not herald customer service as its cornerstone, but instead hinges on the traditional values of education, research, and scholarship? Arguably, any efforts expended on this issue will not affect the annual fund bottom line today or tomorrow. However, the energy spent on creating a positive culture for our current students will have an impact five, 10, or even 15 years down the road. Partnering with the head of student affairs to help work toward a positive culture will strengthen our overall efforts.

The faculty and staff. The core of any institution is its faculty. And, quite frankly, this one area probably has the largest impact on future donors while also being the one you may be least able to influence. In the same way that it is important for you to partner with student affairs, your ability to enlist the support of the faculty is crucial to a comprehensive annual giving program. Consider developing a faculty-staff campaign, or at least a faculty advisory committee. Encourage alumni donors to make annual gifts in honor of faculty and publicize those honors. Ask the president and vice president to help you involve faculty by focusing attention on the impact annual gifts has on faculty research or teaching. Regardless of your strategy, the faculty and staff represent the "front line" to your students, and it is important that each faculty and staff member understands the impact of your program.

Real-Life Points for Practice

Create an influence chart for your organization as a series of concentric or overlapping circles. In each circle, identify the names of individuals who could be resources for you in the effort to change your institution's culture.

Chapter 3

The Annual Fund and the Alumni Program

ALL TOO OFTEN, WE HEAR PHRASES SUCH AS "THE ALUMNI STAFF are the friend raisers and the development staff are the fund raisers." Not only are statements like these shortsighted, they are simply not accurate. In reality, both the annual fund and the alumni association are in the business of strengthening friendships, creating opportunities, building the alumni commitment, and furthering the needs and mission of our institutions. Each needs to view the other as a partner rather than a competitor, a resource rather than a "parasite." Often, though, these two programs find themselves in competition—maybe without realizing it.

The area in which competition is perhaps most likely to develop is that of alumni association dues, if they exist. In general, an alumni association represents all alumni of a particular institution. The efforts of the association are geared toward strengthening the relationship between the school and alumni everywhere. Many alumni associations also develop a dues program whereby interested alumni are asked to pay a nominal annual fee that can range from $10 to $75 depending on the institution. This dues fee is designed to generate revenue to support the efforts of the alumni association. Most associations with dues programs extend an array of benefits to dues payers. These may include discounts on events, access to campus facilities, and the opportunity to purchase services like cellular phone services, rental cars, and insurance at a discount.

The dues payment typically involves writing a check or providing a credit card number. Likewise, making a gift to the annual fund may also involve a check or credit card payment. The important question is whether there is a distinguishable difference from the alumni perspective. If our alumni do not perceive any difference between the check they write to the alumni association and the check they write to the annual fund, it is very likely the two are unintentionally competing.

To determine whether our programs are competing, we need to consider how alumni perceive them. To begin with, there are two predominant reasons alumni choose to pay dues:

- They see a value in the benefits afforded to dues payers and therefore "purchase" these benefits through payment of dues.
- They pay dues as an expression of support for or loyalty to the institution.

These reasons are neither mutually exclusive nor the only reasons people pay dues. A person may pay dues because his or her best friend asked him or her to, or because that person is a volunteer with the alumni association and feels obligated to be a dues payer. However, outside these unique motivations, the great majority of dues payers fall into these two categories.

When the alumni association develops a case for dues support that relies on the first motivation, alumni generally can distinguish the difference between paying dues to the association and making a charitable contribution to the annual fund. However, when the second motivation—loyalty to the institution—is the overriding theme of the dues program, there is potential for the messages of the two programs to become blurred. Alumni, therefore, could simply choose one or the other and not both.

Real-Life Points for Practice

If your alumni association charges dues, identify what percentage of dues payers also make a gifts to the annual fund. Compare these numbers for the past several years, and rate them using the following guidelines:

75 percent or more	above average
60-75 percent	average
40-60 percent	below average
40 percent or less	a real problem

Beyond the issue of dues, there are other occasions where confusion between the two programs can occur. For instance, many alumni associations periodically run fund-raising campaigns for special projects, scholarships, or other causes of alumni interest. While this can be a very successful effort resulting in significant gifts, it can compete with the regular annual fund if not positioned carefully. This confusion can be exacerbated if the alumni association uses phonathons and other "annual-fund-style" solicitation efforts.

These issues might suggest that the relationship between an annual fund and an alumni program is by nature a combative one. This should not be the case. Although these two programs have very distinct missions, they work hand-in-hand to strengthen the relationship between alumni and the institution. They both communicate with alumni; they both create opportunities for involvement and volunteerism; and they both serve as a connection point for alumni with a place that (we hope!) is very important to them.

In most institutions, there is room at the table for both programs, provided that we follow a few basic guidelines.

Establish a clear mission and message for both programs. Membership in an alumni association is just that—a membership. In many cases, the membership fee is not considered a contribution, and it may not be fully tax deductible. Members are purchasing something for their dues. Arguably, much of what they purchase may be intangible. Alumni outreach, communication, and the like cannot always be clearly identified on a list of benefits. However, in the strongest of programs, there are also very tangible benefits consistent with the organization's mission to serve alumni. Benefits typically include use of the campus library or recreation facilities, perhaps even bookstore discounts. Noncampus-oriented benefits may range from car rental and cellular phone discounts to credit card options and insurance programs.

Conversely, a gift to the annual fund typically may not involve many tangible benefits, if any. Aside from the tax deductibility issues, which we will discuss in more detail in Chapter 12, "Gift Societies and Gift Clubs," the heart of the annual fund mission is the creation of philanthropy—the idea of giving rather than buying. Later, when we talk about the annual fund case, we'll examine the importance of clearly demonstrating what annual gifts support through tangible examples. However, aside from the occasional bookmark, bumper sticker, coffee mug, and so forth, the annual fund is not about buying merchandise.

Consistently reinforce the difference between the programs. If you have a dues-based alumni association, do not underestimate the need to remind alumni that there is a difference between dues and gifts. There are many opportunities to do this in both spoken and written communication. For example, look at the alumni association's dues solicitation. Does it acknowledge anywhere that this is a membership, and not considered an annual contribution? Does it invite the alumnus to contact the annual fund at a specific number for information or to make a pledge? It should, and the converse can be said about your annual fund contribution cards.

In addition, it's always helpful to have spokespeople outside of your office. In many cases, a prominent graduate might explain the importance of both dues and annual gifts. This spokesperson could speak on behalf of the programs at events such as reunions/homecomings, donor dinners, and alumni receptions. A spokesperson might also be featured with quotes in newsletters, brochures, and other publications. Finally, certain gift solicitations or dues renewal letters might be sent with the signature of this volunteer. The idea behind this strategy is to have a peer send the message "I support both, and hope you will too!"

Examine the language used in promoting each program. In many institutions, the language used to solicit dues includes phrases such as "Help support current undergraduate programs" or "Alumni dues help to provide scholarships." Phrases like these typically reflect programs by which an alumni association, for example, funds certain student groups, offers scholarship aid to a select group of students, or provides internship opportunities. These are wonderful activities for the alumni association to undertake. The problem, however, arises when the language used in alumni association materials too closely resembles that used in annual fund messages. Remember, in order for your alumni to both pay dues and make contributions, you must create some perceptible difference between the two. Examine your messages to be certain you are communicating the difference.

Coordinate your solicitation schedules. In addition to collaborating with alumni colleagues to send the right messages in the right language, it's crucial that you make an effort to coordinate your schedules. There will be times when a calendar-year-end mailing for the annual fund will arrive within days of the dues mailing for the alumni association. Ideally, you'd like alumni to respond to both requests, but if the mailings arrive too close together, there's a strong likelihood a recipient may choose between them. That may happen because the recipient feels overburdened by the number of requests for money, or because the recipient simply doesn't recognize that the requests represent different entities. As hard as you may try to create different messages for each program, many alumni will simply view both mailings as coming from the same source. There's really no magic number of days or weeks that should be preserved between mailings. Just working together to organize your schedules and allow for as much separation as possible will yield benefits to both programs.

The partnership between the annual fund and the alumni program is a vital one. If your constituency feels a strong connection to the institution, your chance for success in annual giving is much higher. An alumni dues program adds a dimension of complexity, but one that is easily and successfully coordinated with careful planning.

Real-Life Points for Practice

Line up last year's annual fund publications and scripts on a conference table. Then lay out all of the alumni association letters, magazines, and publications. Compare these two sets of communications tools. Are your messages about the institution consistent? Does one set appear to be more aggressive, more expensive, or somehow unbalanced? Is the degree of unbalance OK given the maturity of your program and your priorities? You will learn a great deal about how your constituents view you through this exercise.

Chapter 4

The Annual Fund and the Major Gift Program

TO THE OUTSIDER LOOKING IN, THE TERMS "ANNUAL GIFT" AND "major gift" are confusing at best and misleading at worst. While anyone might understand the idea of an "annual" gift being those gifts that we repeat on an annual basis, the notion of a "major" gift can take on any number of definitions. "Major" to you may not be "major" to another person, and yet this is the predominant structure we use to organize our fund-raising efforts. Most institutions have an annual fund staff that works on annual gifts, and a major gifts staff that raises major gifts (however that institution defines them).

It is important that we both understand and embrace these two separate but interdependent programs. We have already explored the definition of an annual fund. Now, let's briefly outline the major gift program and examine the important relationship between these two efforts.

Programs for major gifts—or principal gifts, leadership gifts, or any other label your institution may apply—represent those efforts that seek to work with selected individuals who have the capacity and inclination to make contributions that are substantial in size and transforming in nature.

"Substantial in size" implies that these gifts are extraordinary to both the donor and the institution. Because typical gift size can vary substantially from one institution to another, we might define major gifts based not on specific dollar figures, but on their proportion to an institution's average annual gift—for instance, major gifts may be 100 times the size of the usual annual gift. So, if your institution's average annual gift is $100, most of your major gifts may be in the $10,000 to $100,000 range, with the highest and rarest gifts ranging from $100,000 to $1 million.

However, the distinction between annual gifts and major gifts is not driven by gift size alone, and it is not as simple as drawing a line at, say, $50,000 and claiming anything above that line is a major gift and anything below is an annual gift. This is because, as we noted earlier, major gifts are also "transforming in nature." A major gift can transform your institution by somehow creating an opportunity that was not there before.

This kind of change is important in understanding the annual gift/major gift relationship. The assumption that most annual gifts are for current use means that annual gifts, regardless of size, do not typically transform an institution; instead, they enable an institution to maintain its mission, its programs, and its standard of excellence. Major gifts, however, are raised and given to somehow have a permanent impact on the future of an institution—a transforming impact. For example, major gifts are given to endow scholarships, to permanently fund research projects, or to build buildings. These types of activities have a transforming impact on the institution.

How do these distinctions influence the relationship between major gift efforts and annual fund efforts? Let's start with a few basic principles:

- Every individual associated with an institution has both the ability and the opportunity to make an annual gift. A finite number of individuals have the capacity and the inclination to also make major gifts to the institution.
- Consistent and increasing participation as an annual fund contributor can be the most significant predictor of a donor's major gift interest and potential.
- Major gifts can be made to the annual fund. A $100,000 gift to the annual fund of an institution with an average annual gift of $200 is both significant and transforming. The transforming quality is in its ability to enable immediate change or growth in the areas supported by the annual fund.
- The strongest development programs are those that create strategies and institutional cultures in which fund-raising efforts seek to maximize both annual gift revenue and major gift commitments simultaneously. These goals are not mutually exclusive.

Although these two types of gifts are distinct and complementary in nature, at most institutions there is an inherent sense of competition between annual gift and major gift programs. This competition is fueled by several factors:

- As annual donors are cultivated and moved up the pipeline to a position at which a major gift seems likely, there is a potential loss of annual gift income if a major gift commitment somehow precludes ongoing annual gift support.
- Major gift staff members are typically evaluated on their activity as measured by contacts, relationships, visits with donors, and solicitations. Annual gift staff may also be evaluated by these factors. As a donor naturally progresses forward, there can be tension regarding which staff member gets "credit" for certain activities.
- Annual fund work is sometimes seen as the first step in a career with major gift work being the natural "maturation" of a development officer. In some cases, this creates an inappropriate sense of inferiority among the annual fund staff. Fortunately, this is the exception rather than the rule; the training, skill, and professional abilities of annual fund officers have increased their role in many development programs, and placed them as peers with other colleagues.

To reduce the potential for tension, and build a successful relationship between major gifts and annual gifts, development leadership must make a commitment to ensure the following:

- *Clear donor strategies.* Tension between the two programs can be abated if sufficient thought is given to the long-term process of building a relationship with prospective donors of major gifts, and if the overall strategy includes the annual fund as part of the process. Giving to the annual fund can be an excellent cultivation tool for prospective major gift donors, and actively soliciting this group of prospects can provide a vital stream of income to the annual fund.
- *Annual fund's responsibility to feed the pipeline.* Annual fund officers will enhance the relationship with their colleagues by serving

as the discovery vehicle for future major gift donors. Any time an annual fund officer is able to share news of a prospective major donor and facilitate the introduction of major gift staff to that individual, the important partnership between the two activities is strengthened.

- *Institutional responsibility to promote dual ask.* The responsibility for "sharing" goes both ways. Once that introduction to the major gift colleague is made, there is an implied trust that as the donor's relationship to the institution grows, annual gifts will continue to be a part of that relationship. The process that accomplishes this goal is typically known as the "dual ask" or the "double ask."

Because this last item is a complex concept, it warrants further discussion.

We use the term "dual ask" to identify the common strategy of asking major gift donors to support the annual fund in addition to their major gift commitments. This may seem to be a straightforward request, but it takes a determined effort to educate both donors and staff regarding the importance of both types of gifts. If we assume that our major gift donors are the best friends of our organization, then we should identify ways to involve them in all aspects of our mission.

In practice, carrying out the dual ask can be accomplished in several ways. The most direct way is to include the annual fund in the major gift solicitation. For example, a major gift proposal for $100,000 payable over four years, might include an annual fund request for $8,000. The donor's gift each year would be $27,000—$25,000 toward the major gift commitment and $2,000 for the annual fund. This strategy is most effective with donors who have demonstrated strong, consistent participation in the annual fund.

Another approach to the dual ask is to invite the donor to earmark a portion of his or her major gift commitment for the annual fund. To continue with the same example, the solicitation for the $100,000 commitment might comprise $96,000 for a capital project and $1,000 per year for the annual fund. This strategy is effective with donors who do not have a track record of gifts to the annual fund and may not have a clear understanding of the importance of both funds. Including the annual fund request in the major gift solicitation enables these donors to gain an understanding of the annual fund while fulfilling their major gift commitment. There is a negative side to this approach, however, in the perceived "discounting" of endowment and capital needs. If your organization requires $100,000 to name a professorship, and you "offer" it to a donor for the $96,000 described above, you will need to work carefully with your organization to determine a specific protocol for this process.

A third approach is simply to encourage major gift donors to consider the annual fund when you carry out the solicitation. While this is not the strongest strategy, it is better than sending no message at all.

So, why is the dual ask such a big deal? If you consider it strictly from a financial perspective, it preserves and protects a vital stream of income—funds that are primarily unrestricted and earmarked for current use. In most situations, you approach major donors about large gifts to capital projects, endowments, and other permanent, long-term programs. If you neglect to ask them for an annual gift as well, you sacrifice that income stream while the donors complete their larger commitment. The distinction is a fine one. Clearly, a six- or seven-figure capital endowment gift will do more to protect the future of the institution than a $1,000 annual gift. But if you create a culture in which you don't need to sacrifice one in favor of the other, you will be stronger now and in the future. As a side benefit, you can create a compelling case for the annual fund if you are able to point to your most generous major donors and highlight their continued commitment to the annual fund.

Finally, and perhaps most important, if you identify a donor who gives $1,000 to the annual fund and solicit that person for a multiyear, six-figure capital commitment, what happens at the end of the payment schedule? Have you clearly communicated

Real-Life Points for Practice

If you don't have a dual-ask culture at your institution, calculate the opportunity cost of that structure. Identify the number of major donors who do not also make annual gifts and assign an average "lost" gift amount. For example, if your minimum gift club level is $1,000, make the assumption that at the very least, all of your major gift donors should make annual gifts that qualify them for this club. Multiply the amount you determine by the number of major donors who are not making annual gifts. Then, examine the number of major gift prospects who are excluded from the annual fund because they are in active stages of identification or cultivation. Using the same approach, calculate the "lost" revenue. The first figure identifies the total possible gain if all major gift donors also made annual gifts. The second figure illustrates the lost revenue you experience by intentionally excluding major prospects from the annual fund. These findings are sensitive, and you will have to be judicious when and how you present these numbers, but it is important to know them.

that you hope and expect the donor to resume annual gifts once the major gift commitment has been fulfilled? If not, then there is a strong chance that the person may not return as an annual donor.

Chapter 5

The Annual Fund and the Campaign

IF YOU WERE TO APPROACH 100 COLLEAGUES AT A CONFERENCE AND ask each if their institutions are either planning a campaign, currently involved in a campaign, or have just completed a campaign, it's fairly safe to say that 95 of them would respond "yes." Campaigns are a core strategy in our development portfolio, particularly given the soaring economy of the late 1990s. We run comprehensive campaigns involving all aspects of our institution, capital campaigns focused on buildings and other construction priorities, or specific project-based campaigns such as for scholarships, fellowships, and special programs.

In each of these efforts, there are several possible roles for the annual fund. This chapter will explore the specific strategies we can use to coordinate the annual fund with campaign efforts. First, however, let us address a few summary principles up front.

The healthiest development programs are those that actively promote the importance of both major and annual gifts while securing support for a campaign. (Remember our discussion of the "dual ask" in Chapter 4.) These programs invoke a strategy of soliciting those donors with the greatest giving capacity for a significant campaign commitment that in some way helps to secure the future of the institution, while at the same time asking for continued support of the annual fund to help carry out the activities of the institution today. These successful institutions also work with donors of all capacities to send the clear message that everyone has a role in the campaign.

The strategies here are broad outlines of how the annual fund and the campaign program can work together. Typically, as an institution gears up for a campaign, it will identify the general approach that will fit its culture and circumstances, and then adjust this approach to its unique situation.

There are essentially four possible roles for the annual fund in a campaign:

1. Incorporate and grow the annual fund throughout the entire campaign.
2. Use the annual fund during the final year(s) to create a crescendo of activity.
3. Launch the campaign with an annual fund strategy to set the tone and pace.
4. Don't include the annual fund at all.

Let's look at each of these in more detail.

CAMPAIGN STRATEGY NO. 1: INCORPORATE AND GROW THE ANNUAL FUND THROUGHOUT THE ENTIRE CAMPAIGN.

This may seem like the ideal strategy, and in many ways it is. Creating an understanding of the importance of both major campaign commitments and annual gifts helps to secure a true, broad foundation of support for your institution that is likely to provide for your needs of today and your plans for the future. In short, the concept of incorporating the annual fund into your campaign strategy implies that you work with multiple objectives in mind. In addition to the goals of the comprehensive campaign, you will be also striving to grow annual fund revenues, increase constituent participation, and create a new cadre of high-end annual fund donors in preparation for a post-campaign period.

However, many institutions are not ready to adopt this integrated strategy, primarily because of institutional culture issues. Institutions that have the most success with this strategy typically have

- a strong base of consistent annual fund participation,
- a history of annual giving and campaign activity,
- excellent leadership, and
- a tradition and culture that fosters this level of commitment from all types of donors.

One way to evaluate your readiness for this strategy is to examine your annual fund giving patterns. First, determine whether you have a program in which donors tend to be consistent in giving every year, with a donor retention rate of 80 percent or higher from one year to the next. This healthy retention and pattern of repetition will help you make a stronger case for the comprehensive approach because most of your "best" donors will already be in the habit of giving to the annual fund.

Second, look at your major gift prospect pool. For this discussion, "prospect pool" refers to individuals who are in your prospect tracking or management system. If you don't have a tracking system, the pool may just be those donors you would consider to have the potential to make major campaign gifts. In addition to any major gift commitments, pledges, or payments these donors have made, what percentage also give to the annual fund each year? If, for example, you find that fewer than half of these individuals participate in the annual fund, then it's quite likely your institution has not created a culture in which annual gifts are a part of the relationship-building process. However, if 75 percent or more of your major gift prospects currently participate in the annual fund, you probably have a strong culture and tradition of annual giving that may support a comprehensive approach to the campaign.

Real-Life Points for Practice

Calculate the annual fund participation of your best friends—your trustees, your major gift prospects, your major gift donors engaged in long-term pledges, and others. The figures you come up with are important but sensitive. Share them with your colleagues, and develop conclusions about your annual giving culture and the implications.

This same test can be applied to your institutional or campaign leadership. If you find that most of your lead volunteers actively participate in the annual fund and also make significant, major commitments, you have an excellent set of "role models" who can provide strong examples for your entire constituency.

CAMPAIGN STRATEGY NO. 2: USE THE ANNUAL FUND DURING THE FINAL YEAR(S) TO CREATE A CRESCENDO OF ACTIVITY.

This tends to be a popular option for most institutions. As plans for a campaign develop, the pressures of immediate revenue needs can make the task of growing an annual fund seem daunting at best and irrelevant at worst. The reality is that our great endowment and capital needs will never be funded through $50, $100, or even $1,000 annual gifts. In institutions that need a campaign and have only a moderate annual giving tradition, we typically launch the campaign first, with the understanding that we will address the annual fund in the coming years. This may not be the ideal situation, but few of us operate in ideal situations. For most institutions, this is the strategy that makes the most sense.

Using this strategy, we maintain the annual fund for the first several years of the campaign. Then we use the final year or two to catapult the annual fund, building on the excitement of campaign achievements. If we succeed, we create a broad base of donors to sustain momentum in the post-campaign years. This approach requires a clear plan that addresses several different issues:

Exactly how do you create excitement around the annual fund? Simply raising X millions or billions of dollars doesn't necessarily create excitement for the annual fund. In fact, it can sometimes have the opposite effect, with the multi-zillion dollar success making it more difficult to explain the importance of a $100 or $1,000 annual gift. In many cases, creating this "excitement" requires a new approach to annual giving that coincides with the end of the campaign. For example, an institution might introduce a new theme, identify prominent new leaders for the annual fund, or completely overhaul the purpose of the annual fund.

Does an effort exist to re-establish the annual fund in the giving patterns of major campaign donors? Too often, we move a consistent, high-end annual donor into a multi-year campaign commitment that does not include the annual fund, and then we ignore the transition back to the annual fund after the campaign commitment ends. Equally important, we will probably have donors who were identified during the campaign and have absolutely no giving history to the institution, and we neglect to develop a strategy to keep them involved after they fulfill their campaign commitment.

Perhaps the best strategy for these two scenarios is to use a high-end gift society as the platform to keep these individuals involved. The gift society approach isn't successful just because these donors relish the idea of another black-tie dinner or lapel pin. Instead, the gift society works well here because these donors had already been solicited by the annual fund in traditional ways (phone or mail) before the campaign and did not respond. It's very likely that they still wouldn't respond to even our most persuasive student caller or our most cleverly written letter. However, during their involvement in the campaign, they presumably had the opportunity to meet the inner circle of donors and leaders at the institution. They now need to receive an annual fund appeal appropriate for their peer level. It is this strategy that a gift society affords. (For more on gift societies, see Chapter 12.)

Do we ask for campaign commitments from our annual fund constituents? Here's an exercise in semantics. In a comprehensive campaign, many institutions count all gifts toward the goal, including annual fund gifts. Therefore, the annual fund is technically participating in the campaign. However, very early in the campaign, we should determine whether we are going to actively solicit annual fund donors for a commitment to the campaign. Many institutions have used the second-to-last year of a campaign as an opportunity to ask annual donors to make a "stretch," a two-year commitment that concludes with the close of the campaign. The purpose of this plan is to enable the annual giving program to use the last year of the campaign to simply send reminders to those donors with two-year commitments, while focusing its energy on new solicitations to lapsed donors and nondonors. Thus, we expand the base of donors coming out of the campaign. The danger of this plan is that if we neglect the important task of stewardship of those donors with two-year pledges, we can actually lose a disproportionate number of those individuals the following year.

CAMPAIGN STRATEGY NO. 3: LAUNCH THE CAMPAIGN USING AN ANNUAL FUND STRATEGY.

This is probably the least common approach. Given the financial pressures felt during campaign planning, it is very difficult to delay the focus on major gifts until the second or third year. However, it does make sense if your institution has a modestly strong annual gift program with very little success in the major gift arena. In short, this strategy involves targeting the majority of your resources and staff on growing the annual fund (particularly the high-end annual fund) for the first year or two to establish a larger base of major gift prospects for the latter years of the campaign. Obviously, you could never "ignore" major gift efforts completely; this strategy speaks to how you apportion the bulk of your staff and budget resources.

The goal of this strategy is to grow a base of donors, particularly high-end annual fund donors, to enlarge your major gift prospect base and position the institution for greater success with larger gifts as the campaign proceeds. Using this strategy, therefore, requires a plan with very clear targets you need to achieve before you move into the major gift effort—for example, participation rates and the desired number of donors over a certain gift amount (say, $1,000). More important, this strategy requires a sufficient "backup" plan. What if you do not meet your targets for the annual fund in year one or two? You will need an alternate plan that will allow you to reevaluate your campaign goals.

This strategy may also involve a longer-than-usual "quiet phase"—the period of aggressive fund raising that occurs before you publicly announce your campaign effort. As a rule of thumb, most institutions strive to have at least 50 percent of their goal in hand before going public with a campaign. Obviously, if the early emphasis is on growing the annual fund, it may take longer to reach that 50 percent threshold.

Your plan will also need to consider the issue of helping your staff make the transition to a new focus mid-campaign. If most of your staff members spend the first year or two growing the annual fund, they will create certain relationships, work patterns, and habits. Clearly, the talents of a strong annual gift officer are easily applicable to major giving, but the work process can be different. This transition will require training, changes in performance expectations, and a strategy to help with the "hand-off" of newly successful annual fund programs. In addition, your volunteers and campaign leadership will need a transition plan that helps them raise the profile of their involvement.

CAMPAIGN STRATEGY NO. 4: DO NOT INCLUDE THE ANNUAL FUND IN THE CAMPAIGN.

Frankly, this is not a desirable option. It is best to incorporate the annual fund into a campaign in some capacity. However, for many institutions, this is the only option as a campaign initiative develops. If your institution has had dismal success in growing the annual fund, or truly has no annual fund at all, it may not be feasible to focus on the two efforts simultaneously. The difficulty may be particularly acute if staff and budget resources are scarce, as you may be focusing all of your energies on the major gift strategies of the campaign.

The answer in this situation, however, is not to abandon the annual fund altogether. Instead, the strategy may involve determined pursuit of major gift donors to build momentum, secure financial stability, and create an institutional awareness of philanthropy. The annual fund may then grow in the years following the campaign, after the institutional culture has changed as a result of success in the major gifts effort.

In summary, the complex relationship between campaigns and annual giving is uniquely specific to each institution. The decision to adopt one strategy over another or to develop some hybrid of multiple strategies is a function of institutional history and culture, budget and staff, campaign priorities, and leadership. The real "take-away" from this section is that planning for the annual fund in the context of the campaign is an essential part of campaign strategy, and it needs to happen before the launch of the campaign. Equally important to the strategy you adopt is the process of evaluating the options. It is through the process of evaluating and identifying options that you will learn how to position both the campaign and the annual fund for success in the long term.

SECTION II

The Annual Fund in Practice: The Tools

The first section of this book addressed general concepts about annual giving and its relationship to the institution. Now we will turn to the specific techniques of annual giving. Annual giving efforts combine two important components: (1) tools, particularly solicitation tools such as direct mail, phonathons, personal visits, and Web home pages; and (2) programs, such as young alumni funds, parents programs, class agents, reunion gift programs, leadership gift clubs, and matching gift programs. We will explore programs in more detail in Section III. First, let us focus on tools and on how to use these tools in the most effective, efficient manner to bring in the largest possible number of donors and dollars.

The principles of our solicitation tools have remained fairly consistent for many years. However, the application of the different techniques has changed dramatically. For example, direct mail historically has been the cornerstone of annual giving programs, with nonprofit organizations such as the YMCA and the Salvation Army having long, distinguished histories of fund-raising mailings. The case for support may have stayed consistent over the years; however, a Salvation Army letter from the 1950s looks and feels very different from one used today, thanks primarily to incredible advances in technology.

Phonathons came into being in the late 1950s with Columbia University running the first large-scale phoning effort in 1958. Following a presentation by Columbia at a professional conference, Cornell University picked up the model and David Dunlop implemented the same "alumni-calling-alumni" phonathon at Cornell in 1959. As we moved into the 1980s, larger programs using student labor developed, due primarily to the significant growth of the alumni list after the admissions increases of the preceding 20 years.

Automation of phonathons arrived in the late 1980s, completely changing both the capacity and sophistication of telemarketing. More recently, the use of the Internet as a giving vehicle appeared in the mid-1990s and continues to grow.

Each of these successive innovations has not changed the core of our efforts—our case for giving—but has significantly changed the way we reach our donors and potential donors. It's quite fair to predict that 10 years from now, there may well be another innovative technique that would deserve a chapter in this book. Part of the excitement of annual giving is in the anticipation of where these innovations will take us next.

It is tempting to move immediately to a discussion of specific solicitation tools, because solicitation accounts for so much of the active and visible work of annual giving officers. However, it's vital to first consider certain common elements that make these tools effective. Solicitation tools are simply the means by which we speak to donors. Before we can do that, we must know what we are going to say and to whom we are going to say it. For this reason, we begin this section by examining two important areas of groundwork to accomplish before we begin solicitation: articulating our case for the annual fund, and identifying the best forms and markets for that message.

Chapter 6

The Case for the Annual Fund

EACH INSTITUTION HAS A UNIQUE CASE FOR ITS ANNUAL FUND. While we all may share common themes of current use, unrestricted, immediate need, and so forth; our case is the set of phrases, descriptions, and images that we use to compel donors to participate and remind them of the positive impact their gifts have at our institution.

To illustrate, let's examine the case for the Parents Annual Fund at Tufts University (as borrowed from the Tufts Web site):

> All students receive some financial assistance toward their education. Tuition covers only 67 percent of educational costs; the remainder must come from other sources. Contributions to the Parents Fund are applied to the University's operating budget, helping to bridge the gap between tuition and the full cost of a Tufts education. Gifts to the Parents Fund have also supported library acquisitions, athletics, computer services, the purchase of scientific and technological equipment, dining hall renovations, and financial aid.

It's quite possible that in reading the case for the Tufts Parents Fund, you find that there are many similarities between their issues and yours. The key is to determine what points will resonate with your constituents, and to seek the input of both donor and nondonor stakeholders as you develop this case.

An effective case for support should include the following components:

Tangibility. This can be the most challenging aspect of annual fund marketing, particularly for education. Creating tangibility means identifying ways to help a donor understand what his or her $100 gift does for the institution, specifically in light of seven- or eight-figure operating budgets. For most of us, reality dictates that it is very hard to pinpoint exactly where any one donor's gift is spent, and the cost and time it would require to track that information would be prohibitive. If we can create a sense of tangibility in our program, we help our donors understand the impact of their gifts no matter what size.

For example, consider Habitat for Humanity, an organization that works to provide affordable housing for low-income families. It relies on volunteer "builders" as well as contributions to fund the program. Therefore, it makes sense that Habitat for Humanity can tell donors that a gift of $100 buys 30 two-by-four studs for framing a room, or 18 sheets of drywall, or 10 rolls of attic insulation. The contribution becomes very tangible for the donor. While our institutions may not compete directly with Habitat for Humanity, we are operating in the same climate of philanthropy, and our donors are conditioned to expect more accountability and tangibility. Therefore, we need to explore ways to communicate a sense of tangibility with our donors, particularly in institutions where unrestricted contributions are mixed with other revenue sources, making it very difficult to track the impact of individual gifts.

Ethically, this can be challenging. The temptation is to stretch reality a bit, identify an area that may benefit indirectly from contributions, and highlight that area in an effort to create this sense of tangibility. However, such an example would probably not be representative and might be misleading.

Instead, try examining your organization's spending of unrestricted revenue from contributions and other sources. Let's say you find that 40 percent is spent on scholarship aid, 20 percent on facilities and grounds maintenance, 30 percent on community outreach, and 10 percent on administrative expenses. Focus on this allocation of revenue, selecting a more tangible example of each area that will communicate just how important gifts are. For example, within the 20 percent to buildings and grounds, you might profile the fact that you have created a new series of walkways and ramps making your campus not just accessible, but supportive of disabled individuals. Highlight an individual who has benefited from this change to increase the impact of this example.

Alternatively, you might help your organization track unrestricted contributions in a way that allows you to highlight direct expenditures. Obviously, this is a more challenging approach, and it requires a partnership with your business manager. Once you have identified a way to isolate contributions and track their expenditure, you can find many creative ways to profile individual areas or programs that receive funding from annual giving, including the approach discussed in the preceding paragraph.

There are certainly other strategies, but the key is to create that sense of tangibility so each donor feels a connection between his or her gift and the impact it has in your organization.

A believable sense of urgency. In order to convince donors that their support is important every year, you have to communicate an urgency that works against the impulse of donors to think, "Well, I know I'll hear from them next year, so I'll just wait." One vital rule to remember when creating this sense of urgency is the deadlines you adhere to as an organization are not necessarily going to motivate your donors to give *now*. For example, claiming that you are approaching the end of your fiscal year does not serve as adequate motivation for a donor to respond; there is no urgency to which the donor can relate. In fact, the perceptive donor will know that a gift will have the same impact on the organization on July 1 as it would have had on June 30 (assuming a June 30 close to the fiscal year).

The one deadline that both our institutions and our donors adhere to is the end of the tax year. While most surveys of donors find that tax benefits do not play a large motivational role in a person's decision to contribute, they can affect the timing of a gift. Sending annual fund appeals that remind donors of the upcoming December 31st deadline provides a legitimate and believable sense of urgency.

You can also create a believable sense of urgency by explaining the following concepts:

- *Institutional needs.* While the close of the fiscal year is not motivating, the needs of an institution certainly are. Explaining that each $100 gift to the annual fund affords the purchase of X number of journal subscriptions for the library, which still needs 400 subscriptions to adequately serve this year's library users, can be a compelling reason for a donor to give now as opposed to next year. Additionally, if your annual fund supports student scholarships, and you know that you need an additional $200,000 to support this year's students, you can present a believable sense of urgency for raising those funds.

- *Unique opportunities.* If your annual fund serves as a "fund for excellence," connoting that the dollars are discretionary to enable the CEO to seize unanticipated opportunities, you can create a sense of excitement and urgency around a specific opportunity. For example, your institution learns that a significant number of students would have the opportunity to participate in research with faculty members due to a large corporate grant, but need more resources. Your CEO may recognize this need and push for raising additional research funds. A project such as this creates a believable sense of urgency involved in raising the annual fund dollars that you could tangibly express to donors.
- *Donor recognition.* While the end of the fiscal year does not serve as a motivating factor, the "cut-off" for inclusion in an honor roll may. Historically, many of the most successful direct mail appeals have been sent in the final quarter of a fiscal year with a draft of the honor roll (perhaps only the class or school of the prospective donor). While this is more practical in smaller programs, there is a believable sense of urgency in seeing that your name is not yet included on a list that will soon be published, presented at reunions, posted on the Web, or included in some other public display.

Consistency. A strong annual fund case is consistent from one year to the next. If you find that one year your case pushes scholarships, the next year you profile faculty research, and the following you talk about laboratory equipment, it's quite likely your donors will fail to understand what they are supporting. This lack of understanding could translate into less of a commitment to giving every year.

This does not mean, however, that you cannot use the "fund for excellence" approach described earlier, in which you present different uses of the dollars each year. With these programs, your overriding case becomes the opportunity needs of the institution, and the confidence in the leadership of your CEO. That message should remain consistent with the individual uses of the annual fund that you promote each year serving as reinforcement for your case.

Creating the case for the annual fund is often an overlooked aspect of annual fund planning, primarily because the assembly of phonathons, direct mail appeals, and other immediate programs can be so time-consuming. However, it makes no sense to place your first call, make your first personal visit, or send the first piece of mail if you have not refined your case for giving. This process involves a commitment from you, from your institutional leadership, and from those who will help you refine your message.

Real-Life Points for Practice

Take the time to write and present your case for the annual fund to your colleagues, your institutional leadership, and a group of volunteer donor and nondonor constituents. These people should be able to agree, respectively, that (1) this is what we are asking for; (2) this is how we are spending the annual fund dollars; and (3) this is what a donor would be motivated to support.

Chapter 7

Market Research for the Annual Fund

IN DEVELOPING OUR CASE FOR THE ANNUAL FUND, WE DECIDE WHAT we want to say to donors. However, before we can approach individuals—whether by mail, phone, or other means—we need to know how best to present our message and to whom we should direct it. To determine the most effective form for our message and the best way to target it, we rely on market research.

EXAMINING YOUR MESSAGE

A fundamental principle of marketing is that you send a targeted message to a specific audience in order to move that audience toward action. The underlying assumption is that you know what messages will activate particular groups. Amazingly, most admissions offices at educational institutions hire marketing specialists to analyze the effectiveness of their messages on various target audiences, yet development and alumni programs rarely do this.

You need to be aggressive about seeking information from your constituents—both donors and nondonors—to determine what messages best move them to action. The sources for this information can be simple or complex. You could organize an informal focus group of people from your target area who sit down with you for pizza and a brainstorming session to analyze past solicitation materials and make recommendations for the future. Or, you could analyze intricate attitudinal surveys that compile both quantitative and qualitative data about your constituents—their habits, motivations, emotional triggers, and so forth. What's important is having information about the ways that best move donors to give, so you can then implement these findings into your approach.

The answers may surprise you. Many institutions, upon reviewing the way they present their annual fund case to various groups, found that major changes were necessary because prospects simply did not connect with their message. The University of Washington went through this very process a few years ago and determined that its alumni were motivated to give for reasons that were not clearly addressed in the case for its annual fund. A survey of a significant sample of the alumni base revealed several important results:

- Eighty-seven percent of alumni viewed the university as one of the best in the nation;
- Forty-nine percent of alumni had false conceptions about the university's state funding;
- Eighty-two percent of alumni believed that small contributions were important to the university's success;
- Fifty-two percent of alumni would be willing to make an unrestricted gift if it improved the quality of the education; and
- Supporting scholarships was the number one reason alumni gave to the school.

As a result, the University of Washington began to appeal to alumni pride in the university, a commitment to the excellence of a UW education, and support for student scholarships. The university experienced a steady growth in the annual fund in the years following this change.

IDENTIFYING TARGET MARKETS

Market research is not limited to examining the messages you send out and the way they are received. It also involves examining the way you define your target groups and the priority you give to each. Research on your donors may include prospect screening and sorting methods to group individuals by giving capacity, giving habits, age, academic major, and other key characteristics. It may also involve compiling and analyzing aggregate data that show which of these groups are statistically most likely to include people who give as well as how much they give, how often, and in response to what sorts of contacts. This vital information can guide you in allocating your efforts more productively.

For instance, before you begin a direct mail or phonathon effort, you must determine which groups of donors (or nondonors) you intend to contact, how often, and with what messages. Of course, it would be ideal to reach every graduate and friend of the institution on a regular basis, but few of us have the resources to do so. We need to break up our pool of prospective donors into groups according to what will give us the desired return, whether that is in gifts or in relationship development.

This process of breaking up the prospective donor base is often called "segmenting." In effect, it is just a way of organizing your records to make the best use of the resources you have available. Segmentation strategies can range from the most basic to insanely complex models requiring volumes of codes and schedules. Regardless of the complexity, effective strategies address one or both of these objectives:

- You may divide your records into groups that enable you to tailor a specific message to a discrete audience. For example, many institutions will segment alumni by decade on the theory that the messages that work best for a graduate from the 1980s will be dramatically different from the appeal made to someone from the 1940s.
- You may divide your records in a way that enables you to use your solicitation resources in a more effective and efficient manner and to track results in a more focused way. For example, if you are limited in your available hours of telemarketing, it may make sense to spend time making a second, third, or perhaps fourth solicitation call to a donor who gave last year while you allow a "never-giver" only one opportunity.

With these two principles of segmentation in mind, you can create endless combinations of demographic and giving variables. Each institution has a unique approach to segmentation that reflects the personality, culture, and history of its program. Here are some of the more common factors:

- *Giving level.* Dividing your population by prior giving level is the most common strategy. It enables you to tailor your message, be more aggressive with higher-end donors, and track individual retention rates that will help determine future efforts. For example, if you segment your file into donors of $1-$99, $100-$499, and $500-plus, you can adjust your strategy and your ask level accordingly. In a phonathon, you might assign your more confident callers to the $500-plus segment, where their abilities will yield larger pledges. For direct mail, you might send bigger givers a brochure that highlights examples of how the institution might use a $500 gift rather than a $50 one. Furthermore, you can track pledge rates, average gifts, and retention rates in a timely fashion so that you can adjust strategies if one segment begins to fail.
- *Donor history.* Annual giving professionals often use the acronyms LYBUNT (Last Year But Unfortunately Not This) and SYBUNT (Some Years But Unfortunately Not This) to classify donors based on when they made their most recent gifts. Segmenting your prospect base into these groups, as well as never-givers, enables you to spend limited resources in the most efficient way. Renewing last year's donors, LYBUNTs, can be the most important component of a program. Using donor history as a segmentation variable enables you to invest heavily in this pursuit and carefully monitor the point of diminishing returns.
- *School, department, or other affiliation.* Again, in an attempt to connect with prospective donors, placing donors in segments according to the root of their relationship with the institution enables you to focus your message. It also enables you to track solicitation effectiveness and adjust strategy when needed.
- *Class year or era.* This offers the advantages already noted, as well as allowing you to track alumni participation and giving by generations. Many institutions that place a significant emphasis on alumni participation have focused considerable energy on younger classes.
- *Geographic location.* This is particularly effective during the public phase of a campaign that is organized with regional "mini-campaigns."

- *Graduate vs. undergraduate degree; part-time vs. full-time enrollment; or...(put your favorite segmentation strategy here).* Obviously, this list could be pages long. There is no right or wrong segmentation variable. As long as you address the two principles identified earlier, any variable that meets your needs should make this list.

Of course, this sort of research helps only if you use the results to guide your program decisions. One of the challenges of market research is the resulting question, "What do we do with this information now that we have it?"

Not long ago, we at Johns Hopkins University underwent a complex analysis of our giving data with the help of an outside consultant. In reviewing pages upon pages of data about retention rates, participation rates, and giving rates among others, we learned that donors who had given for five or more consecutive years accounted for more than 60

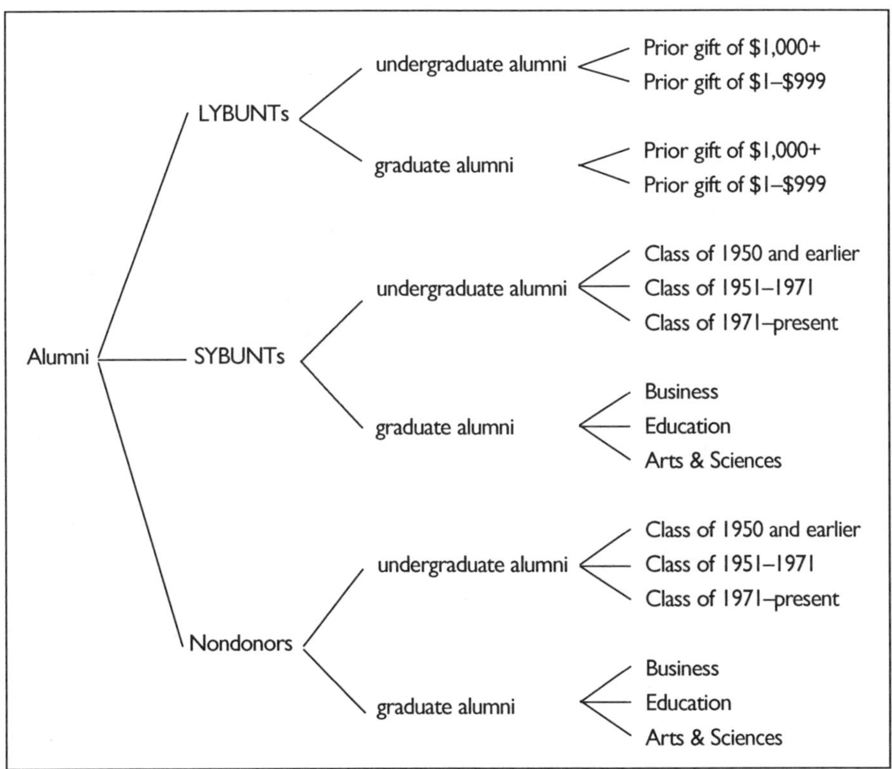

Figure 7.1: Sample Segmentation

percent of annual fund revenue. Furthermore, when we examined donors of three or more consecutive years, we found that this larger group accounted for more than 75 percent of our revenue. It may seem as though this "discovery" isn't really a discovery, and anyone might have guessed it. However, when we looked at our systems, we found we had nothing in place in our phone or mailing programs to address the importance of consecutive givers. Our task now is to design strategies for, and more carefully track revenue from, this important group. In particular, we'll seek to secure our already high renewal rate of consecutive year donors, and to raise the renewal and retention rate of new donors and second-year donors.

Real-Life Points for Practice

Engage in a periodic (semi-annual) review of your segmentation strategies. This can best be accomplished with a large, dry erase board typically found in conference rooms. Gather staff and colleagues and "map" your segmentation logic on the board (for example, see figure 7.1). Then examine each segment with respect to the two objectives previously identified. Does each segment allow you to (1) tailor a specific message, or (2) deploy resources efficiently or track specific results? If you find a segment that doesn't accomplish either of these objectives, you should carefully discuss the logic behind that choice.

Direct Mail

IF YOU HAVE EVER WRITTEN A DIRECT MAIL SOLICITATION LETTER, YOU have probably experienced the "feast or famine" syndrome. There are times when you sit at the computer with the obligatory "Dear Mr. Sample" salutation of your draft, and you cannot get past the first word. There are also occasions when the words flow so freely you feel you could write 10 powerful letters. This experience speaks to the heart of direct mail fund raising. In one or two pages, we want to provide compelling, relevant, believable language that will move a reader to action. And unlike phone calls and personal visits, which give us the opportunity to respond to an individual's questions and concerns, direct mail letters must stand alone.

Although there are exceptions, direct mail is typically the least expensive fund-raising program. It also has the lowest response rate, or yield. The yield can vary significantly, a 2 to 5 percent response on a large mailing is considered successful. In contrast, a smaller, targeted mailing to high-end, consistent donors may produce a 50 percent or even 75 percent response rate. Even with these unpredictable fluctuations, there are several important reasons why we incorporate direct mail into our program:

- It creates a visual image of the annual fund and helps make the program "tangible" to the donor.
- It has a long-term reminder effect—recipients can keep a direct mail response card in their "bill pile" for days, weeks, or even months, allowing them to make the gift according to their timetable.
- With the growth in answering machines, caller ID machines, and other "screening" tactics against telemarketing, direct mail letters are sometimes our only contact with a donor.

- Direct mail allows us a level of creativity and innovation that is harder to accomplish with telemarketing scripts.

The real beauty of a direct mail program is its flexibility. Consider, for example, a well-developed annual fund effort that has the resources to send five different direct mail solicitations in a 12-month cycle. Perhaps the first is a "kick-off" of sorts, signed by the president/CEO, the chair of the board, or some other leader. Next, a class agent letter goes out a few months later, to be followed by a calendar-year-end appeal with a "holiday gift" theme. In the early spring, a brochure is mailed with testimonials from students who describe the impact of the annual fund on their educational experience. Finally, the trusted class agent makes one final appeal approaching fiscal year-end, enclosing a "draft" of the honor roll as a catalyst for giving. These five mailings take five distinctly different approaches, yet all support the same fund. Each one emphasizes a case for giving that ideally will appeal to a particular segment of the constituency. It is important to emphasize this benefit of direct mail because, all too often, we end up sending a letter or brochure simply to satisfy our solicitation calendar and we forget the impressive flexibility of this tool.

Because direct mail has been the staple of annual giving (if not all development efforts) for more than 100 years, there are probably more books, articles, workshops, and guides about writing direct mail appeals than any other aspect of fund raising. Some professionals in the field have spent a lifetime studying the subtleties of color, paper, font choice, signature size, stamps, and every other imaginable variable. Studies have addressed such questions as the difference in yield rates of a single-page letter versus a seven-page manifesto. There is nothing we can add to this field of research by attempting to define a sure-fire, 10-step program for direct mail bliss. If you wish to learn about the science of writing, designing, and sending direct mail appeals, we direct you to the Additional Resources section in this book, or any other suitable source you might find.

This chapter will focus, instead, on the important themes that should guide your efforts as you launch, revamp, or simply continue your own direct mail efforts. We'll address this topic in three parts:

1. Developing a direct mail appeal.
2. Incorporating direct mail into your overall program.
3. Evaluating your successes and failures.

DEVELOPING A DIRECT MAIL APPEAL

Again, there are countless guides from experts who can offer advice about how to write a direct mail solicitation. Yet while it is important to learn about the use of action words and colored signatures, the real challenge is mastering the ability to articulate your case in writing. As the saying goes, "I didn't really know what I knew until I wrote it down." Solicitation letters often work much the same way.

You should be able to state your case in writing as succinctly or effusively as needed. You will find there are opportunities for all lengths of appeals. Perhaps a brochure only affords you a paragraph, while a letter from the president allows two pages.

Real-Life Points for Practice

Hone your ability to express the case for your annual fund by forcing your thoughts into fixed lengths. Sit at your computer, typewriter, or legal pad, and write an appeal for your annual fund in one paragraph—no more, no less. Now, try the same exercise, but increase your length to one standard-sized page. Now, push the exercise by stretching your letter to two or maybe three pages.

In addition to expressing your program's needs, you also need to learn how to present your case for action now. Why should the reader, who may indeed feel very strongly about your impassioned case for the fund, be moved to give at this time? We can all find in our own programs (or in our mailboxes at home) wonderful letters that are full of compelling cases for support, but don't move us to write a check that moment, or to place the letter in our "to pay" bill pile rather than the trash can. One thing to remember: The financial demise of one's institution is neither a realistic nor a worthy catalyst for immediate action. No one likes a sinking ship. Furthermore, simply telling a donor that you have set a goal of raising X dollars by month's end does not provide a particularly strong catalyst either.

So what does make a strong prompt for action? Moving a donor to make a gift now requires that you articulate how that gift will make a positive difference today, and how that same opportunity may not be available later. For example, if your annual fund supports student scholarships, and you know that X dollars need to be raised to enable students to attend this year, you can make a case that every dollar counts, and it counts now. Perhaps you work with a medical institution and can make a strong case for patient care. Annual fund gifts provide for the care and treatment of people who are in the medical center today. Maybe your medical program's annual fund supports research, and you can make an impassioned appeal that you are on the threshold of a cure for a devastating disease. Keep in mind that the call to action must be relevant and believable to the donor.

INCORPORATING DIRECT MAIL INTO YOUR PROGRAM

If you are like most annual giving managers, you can remember encountering a point in the year when the solicitation calendar eclipsed your own good judgment about the effectiveness of a particular mail appeal: "We promised the dean that we'd send two mail solicitations before December, and darn it, we're going to do it." Suddenly, you are perched above the keyboard, painfully anticipating the arrival of some brilliant idea or inspired message. Finally, in the absence of an idea, you dust off an old brochure, lift some of the language, and quickly organize the mailing. In such a case, you're sending a mailing simply because you feel you have an obligation to do so. However, if you are able to step back and think, you might realize that a smarter decision would be to hold the solicitation until a better time.

"Stepping back" enables you to take a look at how your entire mailing program holds together and whether it makes sense as a whole. In assessing your mailing program, you should address the following questions:

Do your individual appeals complement each other, while still being unusual enough to be noticed? Take all of your solicitations from a 12-month cycle and lay them side by side on your conference table. Include scripts, pledge cards, etc. from your phone efforts, as well as any literature you might "leave behind" during a face-to-face solicitation. You should be able to find unifying elements of all of these solicitations. These elements may include color, logos, themes, and select phrases or ideas. However, as you examine these appeals, you should also find in each an element that makes that solicitation unique. Perhaps it's a different volunteer signature, a slightly different call for action, or a different expression of the same case.

Have you allowed each appeal to be efficient and effective on its own without "poaching" from another one? The concept of "poaching" actually applies to both mailings and phonathons. To understand poaching, you first have to view a direct mail solicitation (or a phonathon) as an investment. You have invested resources into an effort with the assumption of a return. Your goal is to maximize that return. In order to maximize that return, you want to allow the strength of a solicitation to reach its full potential. That may take several weeks as some donors may respond immediately, while others may respond the next time they pay bills or are otherwise moved to respond. If a second solicitation comes too closely on the heels of the first, donors who were going to respond to the first one now have two solicitations and could respond to either. Of course, you want these donors no matter what mailing they choose to respond to. But if a donor would have responded to the first mailing and was simply waiting until the next week or the next paycheck, then you have essentially wasted the investment in the second mailing. One mailing has "poached" from another, thereby lowering your overall return on your investment.

Are you keenly aware of the point of diminishing returns? This is the point at which you have reached your saturation point on mailing to your constituency. With each successive mailing, you should be monitoring total dollars, average gift, cost per dollar raised, and so forth (see the following section on evaluation). As you move from mailing one to mailing two, and then to mailing three and so on, you should see a steadily increasing return on your investment. You will, however, reach a point at which the cost-to-raise-a-dollar rises higher and higher, to the point where you may actually be losing money. That point, when the returns no longer warrant the expense, is the point of diminishing returns. It is too easy to neglect that point when you feel pressure to "get one more mailing out before the end of the year," rather than carefully evaluating the effectiveness of that mailing.

EVALUATING YOUR SUCCESSES AND FAILURES

The evaluation tools for direct mail range from simple to complex depending on your needs. In measuring direct mail effectiveness, you want to determine

- If people responded, and how frequently;
- How much they responded with;
- What variables moved them to respond, and
- How can you compare one variable to another.

You can answer these questions using a few basic calculations. The response rate (or yield rate) is the percentage of donors who responded with a gift as a proportion of the entire mailing size. The average gift is simply the total dollars raised divided by the number of donors responding to the mailing. With these two statistics, you can evaluate a whole series of variables within a mailing. Now, you test, test, test. With every mailing you send, you have the opportunity to test at least one variable, if not more. Examples of such variables include

- signature (staff vs. volunteer; color vs. black ink),
- length of letter,
- teaser copy on the front of the envelope,
- suggested dollar amounts,
- level of personalization, and
- inclusion of a brochure or other publication.

The list could go on for pages. The simplest way to test is to randomly divide a mailing into two sections and test one variable. For example, you might send one-half of the mailing using first-class postage and the other half at bulk rate. Assign two different appeal tracking codes (see the list of "Useful Terms" at the end of this book) and compare the results. You will quickly learn what techniques work with your constituency. As you become more skilled, you can conduct multi-variable tests (i.e. first-class vs. bulk rate along with staff vs. volunteer signature). National mailing firms devise intricate testing and tracking grids that may examine 10, 20, or more variables in one mailing. You should feel confident testing two or three before moving into more advanced testing techniques.

Direct mail is truly an art and a science. The art is in the word-smithing of a compelling, passionate appeal that moves the reader to action. The science is in managing and tracking the results, and effectively using these statistics to promote growth.

Chapter 9

Phonathons and Telemarketing

INSTITUTIONS INVENT ALL KINDS OF CREATIVE NAMES TO REFER TO their telephone solicitation effort—Lion Line, Call a Cougar, Phone a Falcon, Dial a Devil, etc. Regardless of the name, telemarketing to prospective donors continues to be one of the biggest tools in our toolbox. It is interesting to examine the last 20 to 30 years of annual funds and compare the balance between telephone and mail efforts. While individual institutions may continue to favor one method over another, at the beginning of the 21st century, we seem to have reached a period in which direct mail and telemarketing are in a very strong, balanced position. We still rely on telemarketing as a significant source of revenue—50 percent, perhaps 70 percent of a typical annual fund may be raised through phone pledges. Yet we have developed a growing reliance on direct mail appeals to reach hard-to-phone individuals and to penetrate our lists more completely.

In the simplest terms, telemarketing involves using the telephone to connect individually with donors or prospective donors. Callers may be alumni or student volunteers, paid students, parents, or almost anyone else. Phonathons may span a week, a month, or the entire fiscal year. We may be very aggressive in our solicitations, asking for $1,000, $3,000, or even $5,000 as our first ask; or we may be more reserved, beginning with a $50 ask. There are multiple variables to consider, which we will explore in this chapter.

As with direct mail, there exist countless resources to provide basic training in phonathon management. The Council for Advancement and Support of Education (CASE) provides semi-annual conferences dedicated to telemarketing, as do many other professional fund-raising associations. Therefore, this chapter is not intended as an A-to-Z guide on how to start and manage a telemarketing program, or where to find the best callers and how to motivate them. Instead, we'll focus this section on the following two areas:

1. How you determine the type of program that is most effective for your institution, and what factors you need to consider in starting a telemarketing effort.
2. How you "perfect" a well-established program.

DETERMINING YOUR PROGRAM AND START-UP NEEDS

As with every decision you make in developing an annual giving effort, the specifics of your institution will help shape the type of telemarketing effort you use. The process of "determining your program" refers to the significant decisions you face in organizing a telemarketing effort—everything from who to use as callers to how to accept payments. While the list of questions that follows may not be exhaustive, these issues represent many of the major decisions you'll need to address. Furthermore, they should point you toward other choices that will also help you shape your program.

Should you use paid callers, volunteer callers, or some combination of the two? The use of paid or volunteer callers is a function of budget and staffing, institutional culture, and the need to control the message. Obviously, volunteers are less expensive in an hour-to-hour comparison against paid students. However, staff commitment should not be underestimated. In many cases, once you factor in the cost of staff time to manage the effort, it can be as costly to run a successful volunteer phonathon as it might be to run a paid student program for the same institution. The time commitment in a volunteer program involves recruiting and training callers plus constant stewardship, cajoling, and reminding. The use of paid callers allows for more extensive caller training, a clear sense of accountability, and perhaps more reliability.

Who will manage the program—a professional member of the staff, a graduate assistant, student supervisors, or someone else? Phonathon programs are time- and labor-intensive, and they require a significant staffing commitment. You have several options to consider, although your final choice may be driven by factors outside of your control (budget, personnel policies, and the like).

Regardless of whether callers are volunteer or paid, most programs require a full-time staff member's time to plan and organize the calling program, recruit and train callers, manage the sessions, and handle all of the post-call materials. Now, this doesn't necessarily mean you need to run out and hire a "phonathon manager" or some equivalent. Instead, make the judgment based on your calling volume. If you have 10,000 constituents and can run a volunteer program that contacts 70 percent of this group in just six weeks, you can probably afford to have an assistant director position in which phonathon management accounts for one-third of the duties. The balance of the position might be focused on parents programs, young alumni programs, or other projects. However, if you have a program with 100,000-plus constituents and a year-round automated, paid caller effort, you will obviously need one, if not two staff positions to manage all of the aspects of your program.

Here are a few variations:

- *Student supervisors* enable you to extend your professional staff by identifying top-performing callers and giving them increased responsibility for program management, caller recruiting and training, and other activities.
- *Graduate assistants* afford the same benefit as student supervisors, with an additional level of maturity and accountability.
- *Contract positions* enable you to hire a professional on a limited-time contract so that you can adequately staff the phonathon season, yet avoid the commitment of a full-year salary if budgets are tight.

Can you handle your entire constituency in-house, or should you consider outsourcing a portion of your records to a professional telemarketing vendor? No discussion of phonathon management would be complete without addressing the in-house/outsource issue. As you weigh your program management options, you will inevitably entertain the idea of sending either part or all of your constituency to an outside vendor. A program might use outside telemarketing vendors because

- The program cannot fully penetrate its calling list using students and/or volunteers, because of a large constituency, a limited caller pool, or both.
- The institution has no strong history of telemarketing, and the start-up costs of beginning a new program are too great. (Don't underestimate these start-up costs; they can run into the $10,000 to $50,000 range, depending on your situation.)
- The institution does not enroll traditional students and, therefore, the annual giving program does not have a traditional group of students and/or alumni from which to recruit callers. (Examples might include many community colleges, technical schools, culinary institutes, etc.)
- The "case for giving" to this institution is better presented by a caller constituency that you don't have access to. (For example, perhaps your constituency consists of former medical center patients and you have found that older, female callers have a higher success rate than 18- to 22-year-old students. Many telemarketing service providers recruit mature women as callers.)
- The size of the institution does not require a dedicated telemarketing staff, and outsourcing is the only logical option.

There are many qualified professional telemarketing firms in the marketplace that can be found on the Internet, in professional publications, and even in the Yellow Pages. There are several important steps you should take in selecting a telemarketing vendor:

- *Seek the input of your peers.* Every vendor should provide you with a client list. Contact as many of their clients as you can and inquire about the firm's success with that institution, their strengths, their weaknesses, and any concerns your colleagues can alert you to. Furthermore, ask the firm if this client list is a partial or complete listing of their customers. If it's only partial, try to find out what institutions have been omitted and contact them.

- *Evaluate at least two or three providers.* A thorough review will ensure that you work with a firm that is compatible with your institution's mission and your objectives.
- *Conduct a visit to the phoning site.* If possible, you should visit the phoning site to see if you are comfortable with the professionalism of the site managers, the attitude of the telemarketers, and the sound of the calls.
- *Ask your office of legal counsel to review any contracts you might sign.* Telemarketing regulation is a growing trend at the state and national level, and your legal counsel can advise you of any vulnerability you may have with a vendor (particularly one outside your home state).

What are the business rules of your program? In other words, how will you process pledges, what type of reminder notification will you use, will you accept credit cards, etc.? The list of business rules can be endless, but they ensure that your efforts in the telemarketing call do not get lost after your caller hangs up the phone. Furthermore, this process is a team effort involving your staff and your colleagues in advancement services (who will see your results firsthand as the responses come pouring in). While this is not a complete list, your meeting with advancement services should cover these issues:

- *How will the institution confirm an individual's pledge after the phone call?* Most programs simply send out a printed pledge card the following day. For some, a sophisticated computer program generates this card. For others, it's a "fill-in-the-blank" form that is completed by the student caller.
- *What information does a caller need to collect so the office can accurately record a pledge, and how does the caller record that information?* Again, many institutions use computer systems to collect this information during the call, while other programs use paper forms on which callers record updated addresses, the amount of the pledge, designations, refusal reasons, and more.
- *How frequently will the institution remind the donor of the pledge if it goes unpaid?* One standard approach is to send written

reminders every 30 days, perhaps adding a follow-up phone call after 90 days.

- *What payment options are acceptable?* Obviously, personal checks are standard, but many programs accept a wide array of credit cards. Some offer the ability to establish a bank draft program known as EFT (electronic funds transfer) that authorizes monthly transfers of a predetermined amount from the donor's bank account to the institution.

PERFECTING A MATURE PROGRAM

When examining your telemarketing program, you will need to note the key areas you need to think about when organizing or reassessing your phoning efforts. Let's examine some guideposts for growing a telemarketing program. Growth in mature programs typically occurs in one (or more) of the following areas:

Capacity. In both volunteer and paid caller programs, you will eventually hit a point of maximum capacity, at which you are no longer able to add callers, sessions, hours, or any combination thereof that will enable you to place more telephone calls.

If you have determined that increasing your call volume is a viable strategy for growth of the overall program, then you have a few options to consider. You might outsource a portion of your file, change the structure of your program, or change the technology of your phone system (i.e. to automate it). We discussed outsourcing earlier in this section. Changing the structure of your program typically involves adding a volunteer component to a paid program or vice versa. That is, if you are currently running a paid student program and are unable to contact as many individuals as required, you may consider adding a volunteer phonathon program, even if for only part of the year, to add capacity to your telephone efforts.

Automation. Automating your program is another subject that deserves significantly more discussion than we can offer here. (See "Options for

Options for Automating Your Calling Program

One approach to automating a phone solicitation program (offered under such trade names as SmartStation, SmartDial, CampusCall, Dial-a-Vision, and others) involves placing a personal computer at each calling desk. Attached to this PC are a dialing mechanism, an outbound phone line, a headset, and a network connection to a main server. A prospect's record is fed from the server to the PC, the dialing mechanism places the outbound call, and the caller speaks to the prospect and records information from the call back into the computerized record. The PC is "smart" in that it automatically eliminates nonproductive calls (busy signals, answering machines, operator signals, etc.).

Another enhancement is often called "predictive dialing," though vendors have their own trade names for this technology as well. Predictive dialing adds one more piece of equipment to the above arrangement—a dialer that serves all the callers simultaneously. Phone numbers from the main records are fed to the dialer. The dialer is constantly placing outbound calls at a pace determined by a formula based on variables such as the number of callers and the average length of a call. The dialer attempts to place calls at a pace that allows each "live" connection to be fed to a waiting telemarketer in time for that person to hear the "-ello" of "Hello" from the prospective donor. Obviously, to accomplish this, the dialer typically has more outbound lines than there are telemarketers. As with automated dialing, the dialer eliminates nonproductive calls.

In general, predictive dialing significantly increases the amount of calls your team is able to complete in any given telemarketing session. Institutions with very large constituencies have found predictive dialer programs to be very effective.

Automation alone will also enable you to increase the amount of calls you make, though not usually to the extreme of a predictive dialer program. However, as you might expect, the additional predictive dialer equipment is expensive.

Automating Your Calling Program" on page 65.) Automating your telemarketing efforts involves adding personal computers, a data server, and other equipment that will increase the productivity of your callers, provide them with greater amounts of information and scripting, and help manage the calling data. If you are considering the automation of your phone program, there are two excellent sources of information: vendors and their current clients. Don't be timid in seeking help. This is a major investment and it can have a dramatic impact on your program.

Your decision about whether or not to automate should reflect an examination of the following points:

- *Is capacity an issue?* If you are not able to reach your constituency given your current program structure, then automation is clearly an option. Still, even if you are able to sufficiently penetrate your list, automation may yet be a consideration, given your responses to the other questions.

- *Is record management an issue?* If you struggle to manage the individual records in your phone program, then automation may be a solution. For example, if your segmentation strategies have become so complex that you spend an inordinate amount of time simply organizing, coding, and then reorganizing your phonathon cards, automating your phone program will eliminate perhaps 90 percent of that effort.
- *Are your reporting tools inadequate?* If you are relying on manual tally sheets to compile statistical information from a calling session, and if the analysis of the tally sheets occurs weeks after the session, you will be unable to address a caller problem that has already done its damage. All automated programs offer extensive real-time reports, as well as an exhausting array of post-session reports that can count everything from pledged dollars to caller efficiency.

The decision to automate is not based on saying "yes" to two out of three of these questions, or any other prescribed response. Instead, the decision is based on your weighing the importance of these areas with the solutions the vendor has to offer and the cost to your institution. In any case, smaller offices should proceed carefully. Automation involves a significant investment and may not be advisable.

If you decide to automate, here are three guidelines to follow:

1. Before you select a vendor, involve your information systems office, your telecommunication services office, and your general counsel (to review the contract). All of these offices will play a major role in helping implement your decision.
2. Allow ample time for testing before you go "live." Of course, we don't live in a perfect world, and many of us have automated a program under tight deadlines. However, you should ideally allow yourself three weeks of testing the data and the system before your first calling session.
3. Prepare for a bumpy start. You will dramatically change the nature of your telemarketing program, so expect a few rough spots. Regardless of your vendor choice, the system will have a few glitches you'll need to work out. Don't panic, but also don't

invite the president down for a visit during the first or second week of a newly automated program.

Program strategy and segmentation. Returning to the discussion about growth in a mature program, the second area in which you can significantly advance your phonathon efforts involves thinking differently about the way you organize your calling pools or segments. This is not a simple task. The great majority of programs have a phonathon schedule that is driven by history—"We've always called business and management in October," or "We always start with our LYBUNTs first and then move to nondonors." Also, over time, you may have organized your other activities around the phone schedule. For example, perhaps you try not to mail the holiday card until just after you've finished your November calling. So the thought of making changes to your phonathon structure (schedule, segments, or other aspects) may thus have far-reaching effects that may make you hesitate.

In addition, even if you have developed a multitude of advanced screening tools providing you with solid information that one group of donors is statistically more likely to give than another group, it can be hard to think about integrating these new codes with your already existing segmentation strategies. You may avoid these changes because of their complexity, but this is the very reason why making these changes can have such a dramatic effect on results: they force you to do things differently, and even to take risks (calculated as those risks may be).

For example, many institutions have explored the idea of gender-specific calling strategies, that is, matching male callers to female prospective donors versus matching male callers to male prospective donors. While the actual results of this kind of test vary depending on the characteristics of your institution, most programs that try this segmentation strategy see measurable differences that affect overall phonathon performance.

The ask. A discussion of growing a mature program is incomplete without reviewing the ask itself. As the first two items of this section covered, you can increase revenue by increasing the capacity of your program, and by defining your calling pool based on what is most efficient and effective.

However, both of these strategies assume that your "ask" is correct to begin with. While a good telemarketing script has multiple facets, the specific ask has two components:

- the case for giving, and
- the negotiation for amount.

You will not make any progress in growing your program if the case you are asking for (unrestricted funds, scholarships, teaching enhancement, etc.) does not resonate with your prospective donors. Re-evaluation of your script should be a routine part of your phonathon planning process, and regular review of your case in general should be a routine part of your overall annual fund planning. This does not mean that you should change your case every three years or so for the sake of change; it means that you should review both the language you use and the reasons behind what you promote when making your case.

Equally as important as the case for giving is the negotiation for the phonathon pledge. The debate about this negotiation probably dates back to the inception of charitable telemarketing. Should you start each ask at $1,000? How many "steps" do you walk down in a giving ladder? (That is, if the prospect says no to $1,000, is the next ask $500, and then $250, the one after that...?) What's the lowest dollar figure you should ask for? Most people who have managed phonathon programs have strong opinions on the answers to these and other questions. Compounding the debate, your donors, bosses, deans, CEOs, and volunteers may also have very strong (or stronger!) opinions about these questions.

We could all avoid endless hours of debate if we simply watched our statistics. One of the classic relationships in telemarketing is the balance between the average dollar amount of the pledge and the participation rate (pledge rate). As you push harder for larger pledges with more aggressive asking strategies, there is a point at which your pledge rate will begin to decline, even while average pledge size and total dollars pledged increases. In contrast, as you "lighten" your ask, starting with a lower initial amount and becoming more passive in pushing for successive steps, your average pledge will begin to decline while your overall pledge rate may increase. In the middle of these two variables is an equilibrium point at which the balance is maximized and the pledge revenue is at its highest point.

Keep in mind that there are other factors in this relationship. If your average pledge goes up with aggressive asking, yet your fulfillment rate on those same pledges declines, then you have to incorporate this finding into the mix. Furthermore, if your aggressive asks secure a pledge for this year, but your retention rate of these same donors declines going into the next year, then perhaps you have been too aggressive.

Regardless of the outcome, the process of examining these relationships between a more aggressive or more passive ask will teach you and your colleagues what strategy best fits your environment. When in doubt, separate a calling pool into sections and test different strategies with each section.

During the last decade, there has been significant discussion of the importance of phoning programs and the increasing obstacles of caller ID, answering machines, and other techniques people use to avoid solicitation calls. Indeed, as you look at statistics from your phone program, you will probably find a dramatic increase in answering machines just in the last four years. Yet telemarketing revenue continues to generate 50 percent, 75 percent, perhaps even 80 percent of the income in many annual fund programs. Until we see another solicitation tool that accounts for that high a percentage of revenue, it's unlikely that we will abandon telemarketing—at least not in the next five or 10 years.

However, we do need to be smarter about our use of this tool, balancing an aggressive telemarketing effort with direct mail, Internet solicitations, personal visits, and volunteer asks. We also need to pay close attention to the wealth of statistics that can be captured in our phoning efforts, and use these data to make smart decisions about the allocation of our telemarketing resources. These decisions include who to call, when to call, how frequently to call, and what to say during the call. Growth in phonathon revenue comes through the constant exploration of these questions.

Personal Solicitation

WHILE FACE-TO-FACE SOLICITATION HAS ALWAYS BEEN A TOOL in our toolbox, its importance and the resources we dedicate to it are growing. Personal solicitation can be found in many different areas within annual giving—for instance, classmates solicit their peers in the traditional class agent role, and volunteers for the parents fund contact their fellow parents for gifts.

But the most likely image of personal solicitation in the annual fund is the annual giving officer trudging through the streets of New York (or any other city) with eight appointments over a 10-hour day, including one each for lunch and dinner. This officer may have no relationship history with some of these prospects; other relationships may go back several years. Some of the appointments may be renewal and upgrade calls in which the officer asks the donors to increase their current year's gift over last year's. Another appointment may involve a prospective donor with no giving history who was recommended by a classmate as a possible member for a giving club. And still another appointment may be with a major gift prospect with little or no giving history, whom the major gift staff had not been able to visit yet, so an annual giving officer tries to secure a first-time annual gift, and provides "discovery" work for the major gift staff.

These scenarios exemplify the typical uses of personal solicitation in our annual giving programs. In general, personal solicitation is used to

- increase the annual gift of a donor with potential that is not being realized;
- strengthen the relationship of an existing donor who also plays a significant volunteer role in the institution;
- solicit an annual gift from a donor for whom traditional methods

of mail and phone would be inappropriate (a major donor, a trustee, etc.);

- solicit a gift and gather introductory information (discovery) on an individual believed to have major gift potential; and
- secure the renewal of any donor (on the assumption that the success rate of personal solicitation is higher than the rate of phonathons and mail).

These are certainly the reasons most often cited for using personal solicitation in the annual fund. However, it is important to distinguish what could be described as a traditional stereotype of personal solicitation from the more comprehensive model that some institutions enjoy. Programs that fully embrace the idea of comprehensive giving in which annual and capital gifts are equally important typically do not use this type of traditional model. In these comprehensive programs, all development officers are skilled in the personal solicitation of both annual and major/capital gifts. Face-to-face solicitations of annual gifts are a part of the entire culture of stewardship and cultivation, and are used universally with all types of donors, rather than only those that fit into one of the categories noted above. Still, because most institutions do not follow this holistic model, we must view the more traditional scenario as the norm.

Because the solicitation/cultivation visit is the primary tool of the major gift effort, some major gift officers may feel uncomfortable with the idea that annual giving staff members are also paying calls to solicit for the annual fund. It goes without saying that the annual giving staff should coordinate with the major gift staff to ensure that it is not soliciting the same individuals within the same time frame. However, beyond the simple matter of coordination, it is important that the major gift officer understand that the two efforts do not compete. Involving an annual gift officer need not compromise the relationship between the major gift officer and the donor; rather, the demonstration of interest by the institution, and the increased involvement of the donor via an annual gift, can strengthen the donor's ties to the institution. We must be sure our major gift colleagues recognize that an annual gift solicited today strengthens, rather than precludes, a major gift solicitation to be made in six months. (For more information on the relationship of the annual fund and the major gift program, see Chapter 4.)

The annual gift solicitation visit differs slightly from a major gift solicitation. You may be familiar with G.T. "Buck" Smith's "five I's" of major gift fund raising: *Identify, Inform, Interest, Involve,* and *Invest* discussed in the *Handbook of Institutional Advancement* (San Francisco: Jossey Bass, 1977). In the typical major gift effort, these steps may be paced over a period of months or even years. In the typical annual gift effort, the last four steps occur during a single meeting, which may last 30 to 60 minutes. Yet the sequence is the same.

In a routine annual gift solicitation call, you might spend the first 15 minutes introducing yourself and updating the donor about your institution. This should be a conversation, not a monologue. If you're skilled in this area, this involves a series of questions *from the donor* and answers *from you*: "What's new with the art center?" "What happened to Dr. X?" "Is your community outreach program succeeding?" More important, it should also be a series of questions *from you* and answers *from the donor*: "What are your fondest memories from your days as a student?" "Are you in touch with your classmates?" "Have you heard about our progress with XYZ disease?" This conversation covers the *Inform* and *Interest* portions of the process.

You might encourage *Involvement* by asking for participation in a volunteer capacity, on a board, or more simply by seeking advice or opinions on a program. For example, with parents, you might ask for their suggestions on how the institution might improve its family weekend activities (assuming they have attended at some point). You need not ask for a significant time commitment, but you can involve parents in the institution just by seeking their input and, at best, incorporating their ideas.

The *Invest* portion of the conversation is equally simple: "Mrs. Smith, I know you have given to our institution in the past, and I hope you take pride in that support. We are grateful for your involvement, and we have such ambitious goals for our programs. Will you increase your support of these goals by raising your annual gift to $___?" Of course, not all asks go that smoothly—Buck Smith's probably haven't all gone that smoothly either. There are, however, a few rules you can follow that will help.

Know your prospective donor before you arrive for the appointment. This should be true with any fund-raising effort. Obviously, part of the call is discovery. However, you do not want to discover that the prospect's son flunked out of your school two months ago; or that the prospect is involved in a legal dispute with your organization; or that a dean just visited yesterday to ask for support of another project. Do your homework.

Know your ask amount before your visit. Many gift officers go into an appointment with the assumption that they will base their ask on what they learn in the discussion. It's fine to modify your ask during the visit, but you should go armed with the knowledge of past giving, the donor's capacity, and any other information that will help you make a logical choice. In the course of the conversation, it is easy to be swayed by observations that have nothing to do with capacity or intent. "Wow, he's wearing tennis shoes and a worn Oxford shirt, maybe I thought there was more capacity here than there really is?" In reality, your sneaker-wearing prospect may be a corporate millionaire who just likes comfortable clothes. If you have not read the research and predetermined your ask, you run a strong risk of "under-asking."

Follow up. In the earlier example of asking parents about family weekend improvement, the biggest mistake you can make is to ask for input and do nothing with it. Even if the suggestion was to bring in a herd of elephants and offer free elephant rides to all of the mothers, you owe this individual, who is now involved with your institution, the courtesy of a reply.

Identify the cause for the "no." If you're getting a "yes" on every appointment, then you are not being aggressive enough with either your ask or your choice of whom to see. When you do get a "no," remember that there are many possible reasons for that answer:

- No, I don't like that project/fund/case.
- No, this isn't the right time for me.
- No, that's not the right amount.
- No, I am not interested in your institution.

All but the last response offer a point of negotiation that lets you proceed further in the discussion. Even the last response leaves room to go forward, perhaps over the course of several more discussions.

The practice of personal solicitation in annual giving programs is a win-win proposal. It can strengthen the relationship with the donor, provide major gift efforts with vital discovery information, raise the profile of the annual fund, and enhance the skills of the annual giving officer involved. However, it takes discipline. For the annual giving officer, it requires placing "holds" on your calendar and working toward filling appointments on those days. It's far too easy to be pulled away from personal solicitation by more immediate problems with the phonathon, for example. All of those problems will still be there when you get back from your trip. Finally, personal solicitation requires the discipline of an institution that has such a well-developed case for support for annual gifts that prospective donors will welcome the personal contact.

Real-Life Points for Practice

If you are just beginning to explore the area of personal solicitation skills, here are two important exercises that will help tremendously:

1. Tag along with a colleague and observe his or her solicitation. As a participant, you should have a role—perhaps you can provide an update on the campus—but your purpose is to watch and learn.
2. Ask a colleague to role-play with you. The more practice you have, the more confident you'll be when you engage in the real call.

The Internet

MANY OF US HAVE VERY AGGRESSIVE IDEAS ABOUT THE USE OF the Internet and our annual giving programs. These ideas are further enhanced by the daily exposure to everything "dot-com" and the increased use of the Internet to handle contributions for political campaigns and other charitable organizations. Annual giving officers want their Web pages to accept gifts online, capture updated demographic information, promote events, present reunion schedules, and more. However, pressing up against this "wish list" are the significant expenses of launching your own site (which involves costs even if you have an in-house Web manager), the long-term need to maintain and update information, the challenge of merging this medium with traditional solicitation techniques, the need to quantify the results with the same fervor you apply to mail and phone efforts, and the dizzying pace of change involving Internet-based tools.

So, given this set of issues, how do we move forward? As many of us are at the very early stages of incorporating the Internet into our annual fund programs, we should focus our energies on the following areas.

Gift and pledge solicitation. In order to generate gifts or pledges to process, we must solicit donors to give via our Web pages. There are passive solicitations, whereby you direct a potential donor to your Web site through advertisements, teaser copy on envelopes, and "click here" connections from other Web sites to your organization. There are also active solicitations that typically use an e-mail message similar to a direct mail appeal, with a connection to your make-a-gift Web page embedded as a hot link in the e-mail message. The creativity of online solicitations has just begun to be explored, and the potential appears enormous.

Gift and pledge processing. This is certainly the most enticing use of the Internet for annual fund officers because it provides a new vehicle enabling donors to give truly at their convenience. In general, when a donor makes a gift or pledge online, typically via a Web page, the information he or she completes on the screen goes to the institution as an electronic mail document. The institution then processes the gift as it would any other, or enters the pledge in the same way it would enter a phonathon pledge and generate the usual pledge form and subsequent reminders. As electronic commerce on the Web grows in popularity, donors' comfort levels with giving online will likely grow as well. Electronic gift acceptance does require an investment on the institution's part, namely the purchase or identification of a secure server that can capture sensitive information (particularly credit card numbers).

Providing information. Web pages are virtual brochures, listing everything from your case for support to the schedule of your alumni chapter activities. You are able to provide well-organized, accessible, and up-to-date information to your constituents in a format that enables them to access your institution at their convenience. The Web is the source of information for this era. When people want to know about product recalls, travel information, and financial figures, they use the Web. Likewise, when your constituents want to know about homecoming and reunions, alumni travel programs, special events, and the new star quarterback, they will come to your Web site.

Sending out regular e-mail newsletters on institutional topics to alumni and friends who have signed up, or otherwise provided their e-mail addresses is another way of keeping your constituents informed about and connected to your institution. E-mail enables you to take the initiative to send information to the person, rather than waiting for the person to visit your Web site. You could provide a benefit to your constituents by allowing them to sign up for regular updates (weekly or monthly, for example) on particular programs that interest them. Sending e-mails may also serve as a bridge to your Web site by adding hot links with your institution's URL so a viewer can easily get to your site if needed.

Volunteer communication. Even as the Web enables us to offer general information to the public, it also lets us provide targeted, specific information to individuals who are involved in a volunteer capacity. For example, class agents at Dartmouth College can check on the progress of specific classes by looking up Web pages that are updated regularly. And James Madison University distributes monthly "Brightening the Lights of Madison," an electronic update of campus achievements, events, and alumni activities. This automated message is sent to donors, volunteers, and other interested alumni.

Creation of communities. The World Wide Web is only one facet of the Internet. Many electronic tools exist that institutions can use to engage and involve individuals regardless of their distance, age, or resources. Wake Forest University recently launched a program through which alumni may subscribe, for free, to a range of Internet-based services. Subscribers may search entries in the alumni database by categories such as name, region, and profession; can register for reunions and other events; and can network with alumni who may share a similar career or interest.

As your institution's Web site grows, you will find keeping up with how many "hits" your Web pages get is a good way of tracking the pages viewers are visiting the most (and therefore are most interested in/ attracted to). If your institution's "giving page" is not getting as many hits as you would like, there are a few different approaches you can take. For instance, by knowing which pages on your sites are getting the most hits, you can make your "giving" page look and function more like these popular pages to attract more viewers. You will need to keep in mind, however, that there will undoubtedly be a delay before you see a rise in hits as viewers become more accustomed to going to this page. Another approach is to showcase the giving information you want people to see on the pages that are already getting the most hits. In this instance, though, you need to be careful not to overcrowd your popular Web pages. Too much visual information can sometimes confuse the viewer, unintentionally dissuading him or her from coming back. As always, the main goal here is to attract viewers and move them to react positively.

Naturally, there are other ways of increasing the hits on your giving Web pages. What's important is to keep track of these numbers, watch the fluctuations of hits your pages receive as you include and exclude information, and reconstruct your pages with the goal of increasing hits.

Eventually, the statistical software packages that track hits will serve us in the same way that appeal codes allow us to track responses to direct mail appeals. We will carefully watch Web visitor movements and build in mechanisms to "pull" donors to the gift page, much like we "pull" prospective donors to open our envelopes or answer our phone calls.

Certainly, your efforts need not be limited to tracking hits. But in the early development stages of your Internet presence, adhering to certain focal points will help you avoid the temptation to "be everything to everybody." We know the Web is a tool of both immediate and growing importance. Our constituents' comfort level with e-communication, e-commerce, and "e-philanthropy" is rapidly increasing, and we need to be prepared to take advantage of this growth.

Real-Life Points for Practice

Sometimes you can get the best ideas for your institution's Web site by visiting the Web sites of other institutions. When you have time to browse the Web, sit down at your computer and visit Web sites of colleges and universities around the country, especially award-winning sites. Take notes on—or bookmark—what stands out to you about each home page, "giving" page, and anything else. Pay attention to things like the site's overall navigation (how easy it is to move within the structure of the site, and how easy it is to find what you are looking for); how essential information is presented; and how easy and inviting it is to "give" online. These are things that can give you ideas about ways to improve your own institution's site.

SECTION III

The Annual Fund in Practice: The Programs

As we noted at the beginning of Section II, annual giving efforts combine two important components: solicitation tools, by which we make contact with individuals; and programs, through which we identify and involve those individuals. In Section II, we dealt with laying the groundwork for solicitations and using the four basic solicitation methods: mail, phone, personal solicitation, and the Internet. In Section III, we will look at programs targeted to young alumni, parents, reunion classes, top givers, and other segments of our constituency.

As we examine the "program" aspect of annual giving, you should notice that each program serves one or more of these functions:

- It enables you to target your message to a demographic segment, using specific language;
- It involves volunteers in your solicitation process; and
- It gives you a vehicle to recognize specific donors in a more meaningful way.

As you review your program structure, it may help to examine each of your programs in light of these functions. During the course of managing an annual giving program, you may be called upon to evaluate whether to add a young alumni effort or a faculty-staff campaign.

The applicability of any given program to a particular institution depends on how well that program fits the culture and demographics of that institution. For example, a school of continuing studies with many part-time and returning adult students may not be the appropriate place to launch a parents program, as these students' parents are less likely to be involved in their education. However, this same continuing studies school may be an excellent candidate for a faculty-staff campaign if it has a large, and mainly adjunct, faculty constituency. Though it may be difficult, you need to be forceful in protesting against adding a program that does not fit your constituency. Too often, we find ourselves being pulled ineffectively into six or eight program-based annual giving efforts that dilute our time without any real gain.

With those words of caution, let's look at some of these program options.

Gift Societies and Gift Clubs

A TRUE "RITE OF PASSAGE" IN ANNUAL GIVING IS FINDING YOURSELF late one evening, perched over your thesaurus like a fortuneteller over a crystal ball, searching for that unique label for your new gift club that will somehow connote just how important those donors are. Affiliates ... no, associates ... no, partners .... How about auxiliary, pace-setters, or circle ... or maybe pals, buddies, or counselors?

Simply put, we develop gift clubs to recognize donors by placing them in a group of their peers based upon the size of their gifts. To be more specific, let's turn to a definition presented by Michael Worth in *Educational Fund Raising: Principles and Practice* (Phoenix: Oryx Press, 1993):

> Gift clubs offer a means to recognize donors who have achieved certain levels of giving. Donors who increase their gifts become eligible for progressively higher-level clubs. Some clubs offer benefits that range from a mention on an "honor roll" to dinners, souvenirs, or special access to campus events.

This definition is particularly appropriate because it identifies four important concepts of giving club use and management: recognition, increased gifts, benefits, and access.

Recognition. The most popular reason for developing a gift-club structure is its ability to recognize donors in what is perceived to be a discreet and appropriate manner. Let's think that statement through. We grandly announce the $10 million donor's commitment at every opportunity because most donors at that level understand the importance of leveraging and publicity, and realize that their peers need to know about their gift. However, our $2,800 annual fund donor may not be so comfortable with the concept of our announcing his or her gift because the expectations among this donor's peer set are different. Instead, we place this donor in a group with a name like the "President's Club," designed to recognize all donors of $2,500 or more, and the donor feels more comfortable with that level of public recognition. More important, we still benefit from the fact that this donor's peers know that he or she gave at least $2,500 and will perhaps raise their sights accordingly.

How important are the dollar levels of your gift clubs? The answer depends on your strategy. If you are positioning a set of gift clubs to recognize donors and provide a "hierarchy" for stewardship purposes, then you can examine the giving patterns of your donors and then model several different range options. For example, if creating four clubs at $1,000, $2,000, $4,000, and $10,000 would place 800 people in your first two clubs and only 15 in your other two, then you should rework your levels to achieve a more even distribution. Alternatively, if you are creating or strengthening your gift clubs in order to increase donor numbers and gift levels, allow for the greatest growth opportunity. Perhaps the 15 people in the top two clubs are true pacesetters whom you could convince others to emulate. Setting your club structure accordingly will afford you the greatest opportunity to demonstrate growth at a particular level.

Gift increases. The issue of gift level brings us to the concept of using gift clubs as a means to increase the size of contributions from your donors. In reality, with the exception of athletic gift clubs, in which larger gifts may mean better seating options at sporting events, most of these programs do not offer benefits that would be tremendous motivating factors for donors to increase their gift. Few donors would stretch and give another $1,000 solely to get a limited-edition President's Club paperweight!

Instead, gift clubs provide an artificial "step" that you can position in the mind of the donor. As the gift officer, you might explain, "Your involvement in this institution has reached a point at which I believe it's important for you to join your peers at the President's Club level. I know you are convinced of the need, and you have the opportunity to join a very select group of donors that form a core of support for the leadership of this institution ...."

When you create gift clubs, you are trying to create a hierarchy that allows you to say, "These individuals have invested in our organization in such a significant way that they are part of a discrete set of people who are intimately involved in our mission." Gift clubs are not designed to alienate the $10 donor. Indeed, in organizations where the gift-club structure is well established, $10 donors often aspire to the leadership level. It's as if every $10 or $100 donor might say, "Someday, I hope I'm in a position where I can support the institution in that way and join the President's Club." Of course, such direct statements happen only in the dreams of annual giving managers, but the concept is accurate. You want to position your gift clubs so that donors aspire to them.

Tangible benefits. The concept of tangible benefits (tokens, mugs, dinners, etc.) has always been a touchy subject, even before the Internal Revenue Service became more aggressive about deductibility issues in the early 1990s. It's very important that you have at least a moderate understanding of the impact of tangible benefits on the tax deductibility of gifts. In the same way that the advice in this book is not meant as tax counsel, it is not your place to counsel your donors on their tax-planning issues. It is, however, your place to understand how your gift-club benefits may affect the deductibility of a donor's gift and your legal obligations to substantiate these benefits to the donor.

To oversimplify, you have two ways to provide tangible benefits to a donor without affecting the deductibility of the gift:

- *If the token gift bears the logo of your organization, and the cost to the organization to purchase this token is less than $7.35 (in 1999; the level may change year to year).* An example might be a university coffee mug, purchased by your office at $4.95 per unit that you send to every donor at a certain level.
- *If the total market value of the gift is less than either 2 percent of the donor's contribution or $73 (again, adjusted each year), whichever amount is smaller.* In this situation, the gift doesn't necessarily have to bear your organizational logo. However, the significant distinction here is the term "market value." The institution bears

responsibility for substantiating what that market value is. For example, if you invite your $2,000 and higher donors to a dinner each year, and those donors recognize that the dinner is a benefit of their membership in a gift club, then you must carefully document the cost of the dinner and determine a market value—the cost for this same dinner in the open market.

Your responsibility is to provide your donors with the appropriate documentation to enable them to determine, with their tax advisers, the deductibility of their gifts. You need to inform the donor of the value of benefits received, if any. *Let's repeat, however, that this is not tax or legal advice.* This is a cue for you to consult your organization's legal adviser about your own plans. As a professional, you need to be aware of the general policies regarding tax deductibility, and you should take advantage of the IRS Web site (*www.irs.gov*), CASE guidelines, and other resources.

With that brief caveat, let's address the larger issue. Donors do not give to an organization to get a coffee mug, a lapel pin, or an invitation to yet another black-tie dinner. Donors give because they care greatly about your institution, and you should design benefits that speak to that motivation. When you think of benefits, try to identify things that directly represent the connection your donors have to your organization. Anyone can get a coffee mug, but not everyone can get a directory of alumni by class year, or a print of a campus scene as painted by a member of the art faculty. And even these items may pale next to an opportunity to meet your president/CEO or attend the opening of a new facility. (We will address such nontangible benefits at more length in a moment.)

Finally, as you think about benefits, realize that you can very easily get caught in the trap of increasing expectations. If you identify a truly original item that adheres to IRS guidelines and speaks to your donors directly, and the reception on the part of your donors is very positive, then what do you do next year? Obviously, one token may not substantially increase donors' expectations, but if you work hard for two, three, maybe four years in a row to identify unique benefits, you may find yourself scrambling to find a meaningful item the next year for fear of losing donors.

Access to the institution. The one item that you possess that distinguishes you from every other charitable organization is your institution. In other words, the primary tool you have for rewarding your donors is access. When you think of access, think not only of the physical access to your facilities or your campus; but also of access to your people, your specialties, and your unique niche in the market. Here is a sampling of some of the more meaningful connections you may offer your gift-club members:

- *A periodic, personalized letter from your president, CEO, or dean speaking about the current state of your institution in a candid fashion.* To be effective, this communication needs to be more direct and open than the standard article in a newsletter. This letter also needs to connect to the individual's membership in a gift club: "Because you are a member of the President's Club, I want you to hear about…."
- *A special newsletter.* To be meaningful, this should provide gift-club members with information and updates on current events, new developments, and other institutional information in a manner that is more timely than the communications to which the average individual might have access.
- *Special events developed for members.* For example, preconcert receptions at which the conductor speaks about the evening's program are very effective for arts organizations.
- *Special activities designed strictly for members.* Georgetown University has developed the Blue and Gray Society Weekend in Bermuda, a program that allows its $10,000-and-up donors the opportunity to pay their way to a resort for a Georgetown-intensive weekend. The weekend combines leisure and sports with lectures, speakers, and other suitable activities. Additionally, it gives this group of donors access to the leadership of the institution in a way that homecoming and other weekends on campus do not.
- *A named lecture series (e.g. the President's Club Lecture Series).* The lecture might be open to all, but a pre-lecture reception could be developed to allow club members to meet the presenter and have the opportunity for more intimate discussion.
- *A reception hosted by a distinguished volunteer, trustee, or a*

particularly wealthy donor. Again, the idea is to provide access to an individual who is unique to your institution, or in the case of the donor, perhaps at a location that is spectacular and not otherwise accessible. You may ask a donor who owns a majestic home to host a reception and arrange for your CEO or some other institutional leader to be there. This way your program, with the help of a special donor, can give gift-club members access both to your institution and to a special place that would otherwise be inaccessible.

Obviously, this list could go on and on. As you should realize by now, we each can identify parts of our institution that have tremendous appeal to our donors because they offer something special that would otherwise be inaccessible. These types of benefits will outpace a lapel pin every time.

Class Agents and Reunions

WHILE IT'S NOT NECESSARY THAT CLASS AGENTS AND REUNION programs go hand in hand, we tend to associate them simply because both thrive in institutions that have an alumni constituency with strong class affiliations. Reunions, of course, are traditionally determined by year of graduation—that is, the class year. Class agents are volunteers who solicit their classmates for gifts to the institution (typically the annual fund) on the strength of their peer-to-peer relationship as classmates. The implication, therefore, is that in order to have successful programs based around class designations, you must have an alumni base with a strong class identity.

Even so, there are different ways of interpreting "class" for either type of program. For example, if your institution does not have a strong class identity because students take varying amounts of time to complete degrees, or your institution attracts nontraditional students (such as part-timers or returning adults), you may have the opportunity to create a different kind of program. These class agent or reunion programs might bring together students not according to year of graduation, but perhaps by a range of class years, a specific academic program, or some other unifying characteristic.

Remember that the strength of these programs lies in the opportunity for peer interaction. That peer relationship can be found in a variety of places at an institution.

CLASS AGENT PROGRAMS

If you decide that class agents are appropriate for your program, your first step is to recruit. (If you have a well-defined program with agents enlisted, you can skip ahead a few paragraphs.) There is no magic formula to identifying potential agents, but as you seek candidates, consider people with these characteristics:

- Consistent donors—not necessarily big donors, but individuals who understand your case for support;
- Current volunteers in other areas of your institution;
- Alumni who were student leaders during their days on campus;
- Referrals from current volunteers;
- Individuals from a region with a large contingent of your alumni; and
- Individuals who have responded to surveys or in some way indicated an interest in getting involved.

Good agent candidates don't need to meet all of these criteria, so you should identify which are most important to your program. In many cases, it's effective to have a balance of many different traits. If you are just starting an agent program, develop a protocol for identifying future agents. One example is having each class elect its agent before graduation. Reunions also provide an ideal opportunity for a class to elect a new agent for the next five years or to simply reaffirm an existing agent. In the best programs, being a class agent is an honor, not a burden.

Once you have identified and recruited agents, how you incorporate them into your program is a function of your institution's culture and the mechanics of your solicitation process. Class-agent responsibilities can vary from program to program, ranging from a simple signature on a yearly letter to a more complicated program with agents actively involved in personal solicitation, prospect screening, and stewardship activities. A typical program might look like this:

- September: Kick-off solicitation letter from agents to their respective classes (or any other group they represent);
- October: Student phonathon for all alumni;
- November: Individual agents identify 10 to 20 classmates to receive personal phone calls;
- December: Year-end agent mailing;
- February: Student and alumni volunteer phonathon;
- March: Agent letters and personal phone calls;

- April: Reunion mailing from agents in classes celebrating reunion years;
- May: Fiscal year-end mailing, perhaps from someone other than agent.

With a schedule like that, we're asking class-agent volunteers to

- Periodically prescreen their class list to identify approximately 20 classmates with whom the agent can have a personal conversation to solicit gifts.
- Write, edit, and sign a solicitation letter that will be sent to the entire class, perhaps twice a year.
- Recruit a cadre of volunteers from the class to conduct a phonathon to solicit certain classmates (for example, those up for renewals or upgrades).
- Make a significant gift of their own to set the expectations for their class. This duty is most important. Keep in mind that the word "significant" does not define an amount, but rather a level within the capacity of the donor.

GIVING EFFORTS IN REUNION PROGRAMS

Reunions provide unique opportunities for celebration and fund raising. On the celebration side, we commemorate a milestone that has been achieved following graduation from the institution, and we provide an opportunity for alumni to reconnect with their alma mater and their fellow classmates. On the fund-raising side, the reunion event is really just a contrived deadline. It allows us to appeal to donors to consider a special gift as they celebrate the reunion milestone. It is particularly effective as we typically bring together class members and recognize their accomplishments, financial and otherwise, in a very public setting.

Effective reunions are a combined effort involving colleagues from the alumni relations office and the development office. Planning for reunions can begin anywhere from 18 months to several years before the event, and planning efforts are optimized when the offices combine staff and volunteers.

If we start with the traditional structure of reunions, in which each class celebrates every five years, we find that fund-raising efforts follow the overall reunion process. If we have volunteers involved, typically, we categorize them as having either program responsibilities (for example, arranging for speakers or planning social activities) or gift responsibilities. The fund-raising process may begin well in advance of the reunion year, particularly for the individuals with potential and interest in making a major gift during the reunion (ideally, in addition to their annual gift). For those individuals without the interest or capacity for major gifts, we typically seek to increase their annual gift in honor of their reunion year. Perhaps this means a stretch from $100 to $500; or $2,500 to $5,000. Regardless of the size, it is the "stretch" concept that is important.

This discussion raises the question, "What is a reunion gift?" As is the case with most programs, the exact definition can vary. As you determine your own answer, you should consider two issues: how you will count reunion gifts and for what purpose they will be designated.

Determining how you count reunion giving is a difficult issue because there always seem to be reasons for exceptions. Your options include

- cash received from class members during the fiscal year of the reunion;
- cash and pledges within the fiscal year (in which case you must determine what length of pledge is acceptable);
- all gifts, pledges, bequest intentions, planned gifts, etc.; and
- all of the above, but extending back two years before the reunion (or 18 months, or three years, etc.).

You can see why this is difficult. What complicates it further is that once you decide on a policy, you will inevitably have a key volunteer who makes a significant gift that falls just outside of the criteria (20 months before the reunion instead of 18, for example). Now what? You may have heard the term "holistic reunion counting," which essentially means you develop a policy both staff and volunteers can understand, and you deal with exceptions as they arise. Inevitably, you will have a reunion chair who is ready to make her significant commitment early because of a unique financial situation, and you will accommodate as you are able. The key to reunion counting is to determine a strategy that is reasonable and consistent. Your 25th reunion class this year will compare itself to last year's 25th, and everyone wants to know that the comparison is legitimate.

How to count the gift is primarily a decision for the institution. However, both the institution and the class must agree on how to determine the purpose (or designation) of the reunion gift. Many programs encourage the establishment of a class scholarship fund or other class-specific funds during the reunion years as a catalyst for increased giving overall. Others focus their efforts on increasing unrestricted annual gifts while allowing those donors with major gift potential to pursue endowed funds or other specific designations.

You can find your answer at the intersection of the needs of the institution and the history of your program. If unrestricted funds are a priority, and your constituency has a history of understanding the value of unrestricted funds, consider pursuing an unrestricted reunion gift program. Otherwise, you may find greater success in allowing each class to identify a project that could be a vehicle for increased participation. Keep in mind, however, if a class selects a special reunion gift project, you will also have to develop a strategy to migrate it back to the unrestricted annual fund after the reunion cycle is complete. Occasionally, classes can get attached to their special projects even after the fund is complete, and this migration back to the annual fund can be difficult.

Regardless of the gift designation, bear in mind an issue we discussed earlier: the coexistence of annual giving and major gifts. Through the reunion giving process, you will identify individuals with major gift potential and interest. While you and your major gift colleagues develop your strategy for these individuals, be certain that whenever possible you pursue a "dual ask." If there are any major donors in the class already, ensure that they participate in the annual fund with their classmates, in addition to any major gift they make during the reunion year. The reunion provides a very visible occasion to profile the importance of both major and annual gifts by encouraging these donors to participate in both efforts.

Once you identify the specifics of your reunion gift counting process and the designation of the gift, you can return to the task at hand: using reunions to leverage increased giving. Again, the deadline created by the reunion event is somewhat artificial, but it can be very effective. As you organize your volunteers for the reunion gift, you want them to focus on the reunion event when individual classes present their gifts to the institution. If you find yourself without such an event, create one. There is little point to having the deadline of reunion weekend if there is no public announcement of class success.

Depending on the size of your reunion gift committee, you may want to assign its members different subcommittee-type tasks. These tasks typically include

- *Participation.* A volunteer, perhaps a class agent, leads the effort in getting the highest participation through letters, class phonathons, personal calls, etc.
- *Major gifts.* One or more of your committee members, preferably those who are going to make a significant gift themselves, lead the effort to identify candidates for major reunion gifts. This would include leading peer-screening sessions, participating in team solicitations with a staff member, or taking the lead in personal solicitations on their own.
- *Stewardship.* If your institution has a precedent for recognizing reunion class fund-raising achievements tangibly, such as with plaques and park benches, you may have volunteers involved in identifying appropriate recognition opportunities. In addition, these volunteers may take the lead in developing specific stewardship and acknowledgment strategies for individual donors in the class (such as personal thank-you notes or a program at a class dinner).
- *Planned gifts.* These are more popular in the 30th reunion and older classes, but are still relevant to other classes. You may develop a volunteer corps that can help promote the use of gift planning tools to help individual donors reach their giving potential.

The activity of the volunteer reunion committee tends to fluctuate. There is always the initial excitement as the committee forms and wrestles with some of the key decisions. The group then tends to settle into individual responsibilities, and activity slows just slightly as people begin to work on their areas. If you are planning a spring or early summer reunion, there is usually a significant amount of activity in October and November as your volunteers work toward calendar-year-end gifts. As you would expect, the activity crescendos in the two or three months just before the reunion, as the goal either comes into view or appears more distant than ever.

In summary, reunions can positively affect our fund-raising efforts in the following three ways:

- They can provide a wonderful opportunity to leverage individual gifts and push for an increase in overall participation.
- They allow the institution to "raise the bar" on expectations by highlighting the achievements of classes and recognizing individual donors.
- Reunions give alumni the chance to reconnect, even if only for a weekend, with an institution that should be a great source of pride and a fountain of memories.

We spend significant resources both in money and staff time to create a weekend that leaves our alumni saying "Wow!" because we know that often the "wow" will eventually translate to participation in our fund-raising efforts.

Real-Life Points for Practice

One of the goals of a reunion fund-raising effort is to increase overall giving and participation, not only for the reunion year, but also for years following the effort. Examine your reunion based on fund-raising results over a multi-year period. You should see a plateau of dollars and participation immediately after a reunion year that is higher than the year prior to the reunion. If you aren't seeing an increased plateau, review your retention strategies and set targets for maintaining a new, higher plateau.

The Parents Fund

RAISING MONEY FROM PARENTS OF CURRENT AND FORMER students can be one of the most rewarding and daunting activities you engage in. While certainly not all parents are paying the bill for their students to attend your institutions, most still are. Success in the parent fund-raising arena depends on your ability to

- articulate a clear case for support that identifies areas that will benefit from parent gifts beyond the impact of tuition dollars,
- engage your institution to create a positive relationship with the families of your students,
- involve volunteers, and
- support your students.

Your initial reaction may be "This goes way beyond the boundaries of my office"—and you're right. Parents are the most immediate consumers of your "product," and they require a cohesive effort involving many parts of your institution. Let's walk through each of the success factors listed above.

Making the case for support. The standard annual fund case of, for instance, providing students with outstanding opportunities and funding much-needed scholarships doesn't always appeal to parents. Why? Because parents can argue that their tuition dollars should cover these items. Yes, we all can point to the gap in the funding picture between tuition and the true cost to educate a student. Yet, somehow, parents may find it more palatable to think of a gift as covering something special in the educational opportunity afforded to their son or daughter, rather than simply adding to the funds they already pay in tuition.

This leaves you with three options. The first is to recognize that parents' contributions do add to the funds that are used for the core process of education, and develop a message that clearly and effectively communicates why the additional monies are needed. For example:

> "We believe that the education your son or daughter receives here at XYZ College is unique, and we hope that you believe in our ability to provide him or her with unparalleled opportunities. We work very hard to keep our tuition in line with your expectations, and yet we know that we add more to the educational process than our peers. We created the Parents Fund to allow the families of our students to affirm their support for an XYZ education. Contributions from parents allow our students to pursue research opportunities, our faculty to incorporate new and innovative teaching techniques, and our administrators to maintain the finest facilities available."

A statement such as this conveys the importance of parent's contributions that support the additional resources XYZ institution is able to offer in conjuction with the institution's basic, unique education.

Your second option is to create a parents fund that supports a part of the institution that logically is separate from the educational process. Some programs refer to these as "outside-the-classroom experiences." For example, at Johns Hopkins University, our parents fund specifically supports student activities, with projects ranging from a new screen for the student movie theater to student activities vans to a climbing wall in the recreation center. In this case, parents can understand the importance of these opportunities to their students, and they can also understand how these may be "features" not directly covered by tuition. Similarly, you might create a parents fund designated for faculty development, enabling parents to directly affect the caliber and quality of the individuals at the helm of the educational process.

Your third option is to encourage parents to identify areas of interest for their contributions. In this case, parents tend to give directly to areas in which their students are involved. For example, parents of athletes may give to the booster club, band parents may support the instrument fund, and parents of journalism students may give to the newspaper. In some ways, this is very effective, as the students are able to experience first-hand the impact of their parents' contributions. However, the challenge is that with such directed giving, it is difficult to create a clear message about the importance of parent gifts because the impact in each area can be so different.

Creating a positive relationship. Every development officer who has personally visited or solicited a parent inevitably ends up playing concierge. As we develop relationships with individual parent donors, we receive requests for copies of class schedules, hotel rooms for graduation, the name and number for the grief counselor, a lead on a summer internship, etc. Many parents desperately seek an open door to the institution so that they can feel a connection beyond what they get from their student (who may or may not be keeping Mom and Dad "in the loop"). If we are to be successful in fund raising, we have to create a way to develop this relationship. For alumni, we have full-service alumni associations. While the magnitude may be smaller, we are obligated to develop a way to connect with our parents as well.

Herein lies the challenge. Most institutions function as small towns, and as outsiders try to navigate through parking restrictions, the registrar's office, or the dining service, they will encounter varying levels of "customer service." Can you change that? In many cases, no. But you can be a catalyst for change. Seek input from parents either through surveys or focus groups. Share your findings with anyone at your institution who will listen. What are parents pleased with, not pleased with, or furious about, and how might these perceptions affect your ability to raise money? Help your student affairs staff see the importance of these relationships, and involve them as partners in the process. If your parents fund supports student activities, you will usually have a partner in your division of student affairs, because parent contributions affect the financial bottom line there. However, even if your parent contributions have nothing to do with the student activities areas, you may be able to inspire a partnership in the interest of the entire institution. Consider the following initiatives:

- Create a parent "hotline" that serves as a concierge service for parents. You may not be able to solve every problem, but you can certainly avoid the call-transfer phenomenon that many parents encounter.
- Develop a parents newsletter to keep your families informed.

Newsletters also provide an opportunity for stewardship and marketing of your fund-raising activities.

- Create or expand a "family weekend" program. Involve your parents in planning "their" weekend. Seek their input on program ideas, speakers, and special events.
- Engage your institutional leadership in recognizing the important role parents play in their children's education, and in acknowledging their vote of confidence in your institution.

Involving volunteers. The most effective advocate for parent fund raising is a parent. Programs that are nationally known for parent fund raising, such as Duke University and Brown University, have established large volunteer structures with parents soliciting parents. The structure for parent volunteer groups can be fairly simple, perhaps involving national chairs, regional leadership, and a handful of subcommittees such as development, student affairs, and career planning.

Fund raising is, of course, a primary role for parent volunteers. However, there are many other substantive activities in which you can involve parents. For example, create an admissions committee that works with your undergraduate admissions office to extend the marketing reach of your institution. It can be very effective when the parent of a newly admitted 18-year-old gets a phone call from a current parent at your institution to say "welcome" and answer any questions. Also, explore the internship opportunities that parents can offer. Transition to careers or graduate school is one of the most important steps parents try to help their students with. Do not overlook the fact that many of your parents may be in a position to offer a student a summer internship, thereby creating a community of parents who can proactively help students in career-planning activities. Regardless of your final strategies, you'll need to balance two issues: the pressure to maintain focus on fund raising, and the need to involve parents in substantive ways with the hope of influencing fund-raising results.

Supporting students. This is where the ball really gets out of your court. Let's acknowledge that when students are unhappy, parents are likely to be the first to hear about it. Consequently, when you solicit those same parents for gifts, you're likely to be the second to hear. This is a dangerous area to approach, because inevitably you will be pointing the finger at another part of your institution that has somehow offended a student.

Again, your role is not to solve the problem, but to be a catalyst. Share your findings with the appropriate individuals at your institution. Try to quantify the impact of "unhappiness" on your fund raising (this is not easy to do, but it may help get the attention of the right folks on your campus). Use communication vehicles, such as the phonathons or parent newsletters, as forums in which you can profile the positive areas of student life. If you have parent volunteers, involve them in identifying areas for your institution to address, and create a success for them to be proud of. In the end, there is a very direct correlation between parents' satisfaction and their inclination to contribute.

Parent programs can be very rewarding. At many institutions, parents fund income approaches the six- and seven-figure mark and has a dramatic impact on the bottom line because it comes mostly in the form of current, unrestricted dollars. Parents programs also offer annual giving professionals a wonderful opportunity to interact with a dedicated volunteer base. More important, parent solicitations allow for conversations with individuals who will immediately see and feel the impact of their own contributions in an area that is very close to their hearts.

Senior Class and Young Alumni Programs

WHENEVER YOU THINK OF WORKING WITH THE MORE RECENT graduates of your institution, or particularly with your senior class, you have to feel good about your long-term commitment to the campus. There is no other program that has such low potential for affecting this year's bottom line, yet such enormous potential for the institution's long-term health. In essence, you're making the job easier for the person who will sit at your desk in 10, 15, or perhaps 20 years (and no, I'm not suggesting it won't be you!).

Let's start with a few definitions:

"Senior class program" is a label that refers to any effort you undertake to strengthen the connection between your graduating students and your institution. It can include activities and programs that enhance seniors' understanding of philanthropy and their responsibility to your institution. Keep in mind that although these programs culminate during the senior year, in effect, they begin the moment students arrive on campus.

"Young alumni" is a generic term that refers to the more recent graduates of your institution. There is no magic number of years after graduation that qualifies alumni as "young," although it's typical for institutions with a young alumni program to draw the line at 10 years. You may find that five, 15, or even 20 years would better fit your culture. The specific term "young alumni" is not necessarily important either, as some campuses simply call these people "recent graduates," "GOLD" (graduates of the last decade), or some other name. This is particularly important if your graduates are not the traditional age (21-25) and may be offended by the label "young."

Given that these efforts involve such a small revenue impact, why undertake them, particularly given the significant staff time and resource commitment these programs can require? There are several important reasons to consider.

First, the adage "habits are hard to break" still rings true, and it's particularly important with this segment. We know, both anecdotally and statistically, that the consistent donors who participate year after year usually account for 50 to 60 percent or more of our revenue. We also know that the single strongest predictor of whether donors will give this year is whether they gave last year. Starting this pattern at the earliest opportunity ensures the long-term stability of our institutions.

Second, in addition to bringing in some revenue, these programs give us a tremendous opportunity to involve students and recent graduates in introductory volunteer positions within our institutions. This is obviously important as we seek to secure a long-term volunteer base with a clear sense of progression and growth. More important, however, is the prevalence of demographic studies that indicate the correlation between a younger person's volunteer involvement in an organization, and the likelihood of contributing financially.

Third, as we all struggle with the challenge of alumni participation, we know that one of the obstacles for many institutions is the growing size of our graduating classes. This issue may not be as significant for institutions that have graduated reasonably consistent class sizes over a long period of time or younger institutions with a younger constituency overall. But it does have a dramatic impact on many programs that have grown at fast rates.

Let's examine the implications of this imbalance. Assume that XYZ College has 90,000 alumni, nearly half of whom have graduated in the last two decades, while the other half graduated over the preceding 60 years. The "younger" half participates at roughly 15 percent, while the "older" half participates at 35 percent. That means the 45,000 alumni who make up the younger half, at 15 percent participation, includes 6,750 donors. By comparison, the 45,000 alumni in the older half, with a 35 percent participation rate, includes 15,750 donors. Add to this the fact that younger donors' gifts are typically smaller than those of older donors, and you can see that as an institution generates increasing numbers of new graduates, the average age of the donor base becomes younger, and participation rates and average gift size both fall.

In other words, as your student populations grow, even modestly, the proportional "weight" of your younger alumni in the overall alumni constituency increases. In the perpetual push for increased participation, this younger segment will have an increasingly dramatic impact on your percentages.

Acknowledging, then, the importance of bringing young alumni and students into the giving program as early as possible, how can you make smart decisions about staff and resources? You have to begin by recognizing that these programs are time- and labor-intensive, and as with many other programs, the payoff is not always proportional to the investment. You may eagerly hire a young alumni/senior class gift coordinator with the hopes that this step will dramatically improve your numbers, and it doesn't happen. One reason for a lack of success is failing to take the time to develop a comprehensive strategy to accompany your newly enhanced staff and budget. A strategy implies that

- you understand what motivates your younger alumni and current students to give to the institution;
- you understand the appropriate "voice" for this generation; and
- you have developed both programmatic and quantitative goals for your efforts.

There are several factors crucial to the success of both senior class and young alumni programs. Let's examine each separately.

SENIOR CLASS PROGRAMS

As is the case with parent fund-raising efforts, students have to be satisfied with their experience at your institution if you are to be even marginally successful. The University of Maryland at College Park addressed this issue in the early 1990s, after years of struggling with modest results in participation and dollars raised. The student affairs division partnered with a wide range of other campus offices—including annual giving, alumni relations, student activities, and academic advising—to initiate a two-year project dubbed the "Senior Experience Task Force." The purpose of this exercise was to gather data regarding the satisfaction level of students and recent graduates, and to make recommendations for efforts to improve that satisfaction. The goal was to increase senior class gift participation and young alumni participation (this was actually one of many goals). The result was a series of initiatives involving all aspects of the campus that would enhance both the classroom and extracurricular experiences of seniors, and also create a more celebratory feel as graduation approached. The significance here is that the institution recognized the importance of a holistic approach to senior class giving efforts.

Another consideration for senior class programs is the structure of your solicitation efforts. Depending on the culture of your institution, you may find that a heavily volunteer-driven program will achieve the greatest results. Programs that adopt this approach typically have a cadre of peer solicitors, perhaps called "Senior Class Captains," who are each responsible for personally securing gifts from 10, 15, or maybe 20 fellow seniors. This should ring a memory bell from the class agent chapter. Indeed, senior gift programs with strong volunteer structures will provide a strong platform for the alumni class agent model. Conversely, programs that do not enjoy the class cohesion creating strong relationships necessary for the volunteer approach typically use phone and mail solicitations as the primary solicitation tool. In addition, many institutions use fund-raising events, such as dance-a-thons, as the primary fund-raising effort for senior class gifts.

Regardless of how your actual solicitation is structured, there are several key issues you must address in the creation or growth of senior class giving efforts including gift designation and whether the gift is made outright or by pledge.

The gift designation. This subject is a passionate issue for seniors. As they approach graduation, students can develop a fascination with how they will be remembered—their legacy. The senior class gift provides them with a perfect opportunity to explore that interest. Many institutions encourage senior class gift efforts in support of the unrestricted annual fund, particularly those where the unrestricted culture is strong. Other institutions allow seniors to survey their peers and then vote on a gift for the class to support. There truly is no "right" way for a senior class gift to develop, but as you help your seniors with the gift selection, consider the following:

- You are training these future donors, and if you train them to support a very specific project, there is a good chance they will continue to be interested in supporting very specific projects, which may be a challenge if your annual fund seeks unrestricted dollars.
- If the seniors select a specific project, you have special stewardship responsibilities to consider. Will the project be completed (for example, will the fountain actually be built on the main quadrangle)? Will you be able to keep your senior donors updated on progress? What if a donor wants to contribute after graduation and the project has been fully funded?
- In some institutions, the selection of the senior gift can actually be divisive to the class if competing project options are equally supported. How will that affect the overall feeling of the seniors at a time when you want them to feel positive about philanthropy?
- There is a powerful motivation about "owning" a senior class gift, and that can enhance your success with a class. If building a fountain on the quadrangle raises your participation by 30 percent, clearly it's worth considering.

Cash versus pledges. One of the basic decisions to make with a senior gift program is whether you will encourage multiple-year pledges or outright gifts payable before graduation (or shortly thereafter). Multiple-year gifts will typically allow for larger class funds or larger projects. Single-year efforts will force you to report only cash in hand by graduation or another designated date. In addition to the size of the gift, there are other factors to consider:

- If you accept multiple-year pledges (three to five years, for example), you will also need to develop an aggressive pledge collection strategy in what can be a difficult period for young alumni. Many institutions have found that, while they were impressed by the size of a senior class gift announced at graduation (say, $100,000 including all pledges), they were disappointed with a five-year collection rate of perhaps only 45 percent on those pledges. Furthermore, young alumni tend to move almost annually in those first four or five years, making it even more challenging to remind them of outstanding pledges.

- If you use a "cash by graduation" approach, you will need to think carefully about stewardship issues at graduation. In other words, if the seniors have all paid their gifts, has the ground been broken for the fountain, or can you hold up the first book that was purchased with the book fund? Can they see and feel the benefit of the gifts?
- Multiple-year pledges made by seniors for a specific project (as opposed to the unrestricted annual fund) also exacerbate the challenge of "converting" those donors to the annual fund after their pledge is completed. If an alumnus has been giving to the fountain fund for five years, you may have to be very diligent in explaining the unrestricted annual fund to him or her later.

YOUNG ALUMNI PROGRAMS

Young alumni efforts are even less "formulaic" than senior class programs. Developing a young alumni program requires determining what, why, how, and when.

What. Exactly what is a young alumni program? Is it simply a different color letterhead with a flashier logo? Ideally, a young alumni program is an effort that seeks to connect with a very important constituency in a unique way during a time in which their pattern of long-term involvement with your institution is beginning to develop. This can take the form of a young alumni advisory committee that seeks to involve as many alumni as possible, or it might be a series of social activities designed to continue the affection a young alumnus might feel upon graduation. It may involve service projects, or be designed around regional fund-raising organizations that bring your annual fund message "closer to home." Regardless of the structure, it is important to define what you're going to do to strengthen that connection.

Why. As with every part of annual giving, a clear articulation of your goals is very important with young alumni efforts. You must determine whether you are seeking, for example, increased participation overall, increased total giving, and/or a larger volunteer presence. Given the enthusiasm of young alumni and their passion for their educational experiences (and their relative naiveté on how your programs work), they can occupy a great deal of staff time with wonderful ideas and new projects. Keeping focus on your "why" will allow you to prioritize the interests and enthusiasm of this group.

How. Once you have determined what your strategy is going to be, you must then determine how you are going to accomplish it. If your project involves a regionally based structure of eight young alumni committees that are involved in social activities, fund raising, and career mentoring, it will obviously require a significant staff support component. However, if your young alumni efforts simply involve 10 class volunteers who provide the majority of the leadership for the class and its activities, the staffing requirements may not be as significant.

When. Just as seniors graduate from college, your young alumni will reach a point at which they need to "graduate" on to the next level of involvement in your institution. It's important to develop a transition strategy so that volunteers, donors, and others involved in your young alumni efforts do not feel abandoned at the completion of that "young alumni" period.

Real-Life Points for Practice

Identify the year in which half of your alumni base have graduated before and half after. Compare the participation rates of these two halves. Be aware of the "weight" of the younger classes, particularly the most recently graduated class.

Given all of these issues and others that you may identify, it's easy to understand why institutions may not place senior gift and young alumni programs at the top of their priority list. They are labor-intensive, and this year's efforts may not have a significant impact on this year's revenue. However, many institutions identify donors and volunteers at a young age, involve them in young alumni efforts, and successfully transition them to increasing roles and heightened commitment. These success stories are the reason we spend the time and energy on seniors and young alumni.

Other Programs

THIS LIST OF "OTHER PROGRAMS" COULD GO ON FOR CHAPTERS—because for each unique constituency that we work with, we have the opportunity to create a program to reach that group. This final section will address some of those constituencies.

Including a program in this chapter does not imply that it is of lesser importance than those covered in earlier chapters; it simply means these programs are not as prevalent in all institutions, or that the details surrounding these efforts are not as complex as those already discussed.

FACULTY-STAFF EFFORTS

"I gave at the office ... and my institution is better because of it." The percentage of faculty and staff who make annual contributions can be a factor when an institution applies for foundation grants, appeals to local organizations, and even approaches individual donors about major gift commitments. It is an indication of your own "family's" commitment, not only to the mission of your organization, but also to the philanthropic spirit that is the cornerstone of your success.

Success factors for a strong faculty and staff effort include

- endorsement from the entire leadership of the organization;
- strong volunteer leadership from peers who represent multiple levels within the organization;
- the opportunity to allow faculty and staff to direct their contributions to areas closest to them, if possible;
- the avoidance of "heavy-handed" solicitation techniques involving managers, payroll agents, or any other inappropriate individuals;

- in some cases, a "retirees" solicitation in addition to solicitation of current faculty and staff; and
- a conversation with your general counsel's office to determine whether you are allowed to solicit unionized, hourly, and similar employee groups.

Finally, you need to establish a very attentive stewardship program. Many of your faculty and staff donors will feel that they already give every day through their work responsibilities. Your job will be to reaffirm the importance of their charitable contributions.

CORPORATE MATCHING GIFT PROGRAMS

This concept, while distinctly American, has a growing application for all fund-raising programs, as more U.S. corporations expand their global presence and hire alumni and friends of campuses worldwide. The concept is straightforward: Companies "match" the charitable contributions of their employees to institutions that meet certain broad criteria. The goal is both to encourage the culture of philanthropy in their organization, and to extend the company's own philanthropy as a benefit to employees.

From the recipient organization's perspective, a matching gift program is a wonderful income source that really only requires three steps:

1. Carefully tracking alumni and friends to ensure you have accurate information on individuals who are employed by matching gift companies,
2. Encouraging this unique group of constituents (individuals employed by matching gift companies) to give, and
3. Ensuring that individuals at matching gift companies who do give take the appropriate steps to have their gift matched.

Institutions have developed many different programs to support these three steps. A simple matching gifts program might consist of

- Adding a matching gift message to materials such as direct mail letters, contribution cards, and phonathon pledge forms: "If you work at an organization that matches charitable contributions, please take the appropriate steps to have this gift matched."

- "Flagging" individuals who work at matching gift companies so their mail and phone appeals carry a special, targeted message.
- Recognizing donors at a gift level that includes their match. For instance, if your President's Club recognizes donors at $1,000, include a $500 donor who secured a corporate match.
- Sending brochures that list matching gift companies to all donors so they can determine whether their company matches. These brochures are available from CASE and other organizations.

A more complex program might involve recruiting a network of "corporate agent" volunteers who work at matching gift companies. These volunteers can help you by

- soliciting other alumni at their organization,
- helping you maintain the accuracy of your database by updating the list of alumni employed by their company, and
- organizing special events to raise the profile of your institution within the company (receptions, etc.).

In some cases, your corporate agent can even engage senior executives in the company to temporarily raise the matching gift ratio for alumni of your institution in order to serve as a catalyst for participation and giving. Obviously, this requires a strong connection with a key decision maker in the organization, and it does not happen often.

It is difficult to compare your success in matching gifts against that of other institutions. For example, the University of Michigan is an enormous institution with a large alumni base. Many of its alumni are employed at major corporations and the university consistently falls among the top five higher education recipients of matching gift dollars in the United States. On the other hand, a small, liberal arts college may not have many alumni who pursue careers within matching gift corporations, and it would have a smaller alumni base to begin with. Therefore, a straight dollar-to-dollar comparison is not relevant.

Robert Caldwell, now director of the Dartmouth Alumni Fund, and Julie Brown, director of annual giving programs at the University of

Michigan, presented a more useful comparison tool several years ago. This involves taking the ratio of gifts received from individuals to matching gift dollars to produce a number that illustrates: "For every $___ we receive from individuals, we receive $___ in matching gifts."

For example, suppose XYZ institution received $6.9 million in gifts from individuals last year, and $338,000 in matching gifts. Dividing the first number by the second yields 20.4. That means, for every $20.40 XYZ receives in individual gifts, it receives $1 in matching gifts.

Real-Life Points for Practice

To calculate the ratio of gifts your institution received from individuals and gifts received through matching gifts, divide the dollar figure received from individuals by the dollar figure received through matching gifts. Once you have this ratio, compare it to those of your peers to get a sense of your success. Once you identify other institutions that are more successful, you can emulate their strategies.

There are also software products on the market (GiftPlus from HEP, Inc., to name one) that enable you to screen your giving database against a database of all matching gift companies and their subsidiaries. This can help you identify where you are "missing" potential matching dollars.

Other resources are CASE's *Matching Gift Details* and Matching Gift Leaflet series. *Matching Gift Details* is a directory, updated annually, with information on companies that match their employees' gifts to colleges and universities, elementary and secondary schools, nonprofit cultural organizations, public television and radio, hospitals, or health and community service organizations. The directory contains 28 different types of information on these employers, including gift minimums and maximums, gift ratios, and company contacts to name a few. CASE's Matching Gift Leaflet series consists of cost-effective direct-mail inserts that instantly show your donors and prospects if their employers match their gifts. These leaflets are available for four constituencies: higher education, elementary and secondary schools, nonprofit cultural organizations, and nonprofit community service organizations.

Unlike funds in more traditional programs, matching gift dollars cannot grow independently—they correlate to your overall giving results. Assuming you are doing the "basics" of encouraging donors to have their gifts matched, as overall giving goes up, the potential for increasing matching gift revenue rises as well. The opposite is also true. In other words, do not attempt to double your annual fund by relying on increased matching gifts!

CORPORATE ANNUAL GIVING

Although it sounds similar to corporate matching gift programs, corporate annual giving is a completely different effort. It is the process of raising annual contributions from companies, businesses, and organizations in your area. Typically, these programs are found in smaller communities where the connection between local businesses and the college, university, or organization is much stronger. While it's not impossible to develop a corporate/business annual giving program in a large, metropolitan area, it is complicated by the fact that a city like Boston or New York has such an overwhelming number of educational institutions and other nonprofits that local businesses would be unable to give to all and would find it difficult to select only a few.

Corporate/business annual giving efforts typically take two approaches. In one, annual, charitable contributions are made much as individual donors make their annual gifts. The organization cultivates donor businesses; many of the solicitations occur in a face-to-face meeting/environment; and, as with individuals, the organization's stewardship is very important. Institutions have developed many names to market this process, such as "Community Partnerships" or "Business Friends."

An alternative approach is to promote business sponsorships of certain organizational activities. Nonprofit organizations outside of the educational arena tend to excel in this area. Sponsorships might include underwriting dinners, golf tournaments, homecoming tents, and festivals. For the business, this is as much a marketing expense as it is a contribution, so you and your legal counsel should negotiate that detail to determine whether the IRS would consider the sponsorship a charitable contribution.

Regardless of the structure of your program, the relationship with local business in your area can be crucial and should not be overlooked as you develop new programs or expand current ones.

NONAFFILIATED DONOR EFFORTS

Every organization has a unique blend of constituents, some of whom may be useful to target for an annual giving effort. Consider this a "catch-all" list of such possibilities:

- library borrowers and patrons,
- season subscribers to performing arts facilities,
- athletic season-ticket holders,
- community leaders,
- grateful patients in both academic and nonacademic medical centers, and
- widows and widowers of alumni or friends.

This list will vary for each institution, but in each case, you are targeting a group of potential donors that has no other relationship to the organization. Keep in mind that there are programs whose entire annual giving effort would involve one of these groups—for instance, a civic opera company would rely almost exclusively on its box office list for solicitation purposes. However, institutions for which these groups are secondary to the main constituency may find it worthwhile to strengthen the relationship and increase the likelihood of a contribution. For example, if you represent a college or university and can identify library users who are otherwise unaffiliated with your campus, begin a directed cultivation effort. Include these individuals in your library events, notify them of special readings and presentations, and communicate with them about the library to enhance their relationship with your facility. You are now in a much stronger position to solicit these individuals and illustrate the strong correlation between their support and the programs they have come to enjoy.

Raising funds from grateful patients of a medical center or clinic is a discipline unto itself. We know that the relationship between a patient and a health institution is very emotional (in both positive and negative ways) and very fleeting. The outstanding medical fund-raising programs are those that solicit patients as soon as possible after the care has been provided, and continually reinforce and remind donors of their gifts' role in successfully advancing patient care and research.

Whether you are working with patients or library borrowers, the challenge for you is to identify these unaffiliated constituents, analyze their true potential, and develop sound strategies that pursue those segments that warrant the effort.

SECTION IV

Annual Fund Planning and Strategy

Somewhere between writing a phonathon script and reaching your million-dollar annual fund goal, lies the process of planning and evaluating. You may have developed the world's most compelling direct mail package, but if it is not coupled with an effective operating plan, it will not reach its full potential. The operating plan enables you to balance your solicitations throughout the year to make the most efficient use of your resources and maximize the revenue to your institution. It addresses timing, quantities, events, individual constituencies, special programs, and more. It also identifies how you will evaluate the success of your program.

The planning and evaluating process is driven by the manager of the annual giving effort, but involves everyone on the staff as well as colleagues in other areas of development and alumni relations, technical experts in information systems, and interested volunteers. This section will give you an overview of how to plan and evaluate to improve the process at your institution.

The Planning Cycle

REDUCED TO ITS MOST SIMPLE DEFINITION, ANNUAL GIVING IS all about acquiring, renewing, and upgrading donors. All of your fancy segmentation strategies and high-profile volunteer programs are, at their core, about these three activities. Therefore, your planning efforts should also have these three actions at their core. The planning process involves a careful review of past years with an eye toward growth in certain areas. The end product of the planning process is a document that will serve as your work plan for the year with details that should include

- segmentation strategies;
- mail and phone solicitation dates;
- programmatic time lines (when to start planning for family weekend, when to schedule the first meeting of the gift society committee, etc.);
- quantitative and qualitative targets for each program;
- individual staff responsibilities and goals; and
- back-up plans.

In general, there are two types of planning you undertake in the annual fund. Each year, you go through the process of planning for next year. For programs that run on a July 1 to June 30 fiscal year, the planning process typically begins on January 1, and develops over the next six months before the start of the new fiscal year. (Obviously, if your fiscal year starts on a different date, adjust this timetable accordingly.) Let's refer to this type of planning as "regular planning." This annual process incorporates analysis, goalsetting, and timetables for regular annual fund solicitations and programs.

The second type of planning involves a much more detailed effort in which you research peer programs, develop long-term goals, secure new funding, add staff, and so forth. We'll label this type of planning "growth planning." Growth planning occurs when something or someone prompts you, the manager, to do more.

What do we mean by this? Here's an example. Most annual funds grow at a rate of 3 percent, 4 percent, at best even 10 percent in any given year barring any outside interferences such as stock market slowdowns or institutional crises. As you proceed from year to year and go through the process of regular planning, you can rightly expect revenue increases in the range of 3 to 10 percent. Suppose, however, that the CEO arrives in your office and announces that he or she wants to see a 30 percent increase in revenue in the next three fiscal years. After your breathing steadies, you now enter the growth planning stage, because you're not going to grow 30 percent with only a routine review of last year's program.

Let's explore these two types of planning in greater detail.

REGULAR PLANNING

To repeat, regular planning involves

- examining the results of one year's efforts,
- comparing it to internal and external benchmarks,
- making adjustments or enhancements, and
- developing the work plan for the year ahead.

As you examine the results of one year's efforts, you might identify hundreds of statistics that would provide insight on the performance of your programs. One of the true challenges in annual giving management is separating statistics that are truly meaningful from those that are aberrations based on other factors.

To use a simple example, assume you are comparing this year's phonathon figures to last year's. As you study the numbers, you observe that your nursing school alumni responded with a considerably lower pledge rate than last year, and the total dollars pledged fell by nearly $15,000. At first glance, this is alarming. However, expert annual giving manager that you are, you check back through your overall fund-raising figures and recall that, this year, you tried a lead solicitation from your president that was mailed two full months before the phonathon. Nursing school alumni gave nearly $30,000 in response to that kick-off mailing, and a great number of donors who have given through the phonathon responded to the president's mailing instead. Obviously, your net gain is $15,000, despite a phonathon statistic that might have been alarming out of context.

Admittedly, this is an oversimplified example. However, this type of interdependence is a routine component of annual fund statistics. It constantly requires you to ask "What might have affected this number, and where can I find supporting figures?"

At the base of each performance number is a "driving statistic." A driving statistic is a performance figure that causes other figures to reflect changes that are occurring in that driving statistic. For example, if your total revenue from a mailing is lower than last year (or perhaps lower than a projection you made for this year), you may chart the following path:

- Total revenue raised by mailing is low by $35,000.
- Number of gifts received is at projected target of 1,100.
- The mailing was divided into three segments: LYBUNTs, SYBUNTs, and nondonors.
- Response rate for all segments was at target of 35 percent, 20 percent, and 4 percent, respectively.
- Average gift for SYBUNTs and nondonors was at target, but the average gift for LYBUNTs was low. Projected was $125, actual was $60.

As you continue your analysis, you determine that the $35,000 deficit is the result of the lower-than-expected average gift from LYBUNTs. That is your "driving statistic" for the overall deficit of the mailing.

The point here is not to complicate a fairly straightforward discussion of planning, but instead to illustrate one of the more difficult aspects. As more and more statistics become available to you, your challenge will be to find those drivers so you can make adjustments or change strategies in the future. In the previous example, perhaps the adjustment is that your LYBUNTs do not maintain their optimal average gift without the personal attention of a phonathon call. Regardless, the key is to react to drivers and not other statistics affected by the drivers. If you had scrapped the entire mailing simply because of the $35,000 deficit, you may have eliminated a solicitation that worked effectively for SYBUNTs and nondonors.

After successfully navigating the world of statistical drivers, what you should have is a clear picture of what worked well last year and what didn't. Envision a chart of last year's solicitations with the successful efforts highlighted in green, and the poor performers highlighted in blue. This may be where you make notes about each blue-highlighted solicitation and what changes might be appropriate. The structure of this step should meet your own needs, but you should be able to identify the performers and the weak links.

For many programs, the next step involves a quick *comparison to internal and external benchmarks*—for example, last year's numbers or statistics from a peer institution. Regardless of the source, the purpose is to double-check your data against reliable benchmarks. If you wonder why the average gift to a mailing seems low, check your performance in past years with that same segment. Perhaps you'll find that there are historical numbers that reinforce your instinct to question this statistic, or that the segment has always had a relatively low average gift.

Furthermore, you can turn to peer institutions for benchmarking figures. You may find such numbers in publications like the Council for Aid to Education reports, or perhaps you have developed a peer network through which you can obtain figures with a few quick phone calls. A word of caution: It is very rare that any two institutions organize their programs in exactly the same way. If you contact peer program "A" and ask about its young alumni average gift, you may find that institution defines young alumni slightly differently, and its statistics are affected by that different interpretation. While there is still much to learn from peers with similar programs, it is a mistake to make blind assumptions based on data that don't provide a true comparison.

Once you have compiled all of your statistics and made the appropriate comparisons to internal and external benchmarks, you are ready to make adjustments and enhancements based on your findings. Referring back to an earlier example, one adjustment you may recommend is that all LYBUNTs are contacted first through your telemarketing efforts so as not to risk lost revenue through the lower average gift you experienced from a direct mail appeal last year. This process of making adjustments and enhancements may be very simple with just a few "tweaks" to certain segments. Or it may be in-depth, requiring the exploration of whether an entire program (such as matching gift agents or a gift club board of volunteers) is still viable.

The final step in the planning process is to *develop your work plan for the year ahead.* This is where the details become a very personal choice. Some annual giving teams successfully map out every day of every month of each fiscal year with detail that would exhaust the average person. Other teams (and yes, a "team" can be one person!) prefer to keep their work plans very brief with only the most essential dates, goals, and targets. Either approach can be effective. The key is that both include the following crucial details:

- *Specific strategies.* It's not enough to simply state, "increase average gift" or "grow parents fund" as your strategy. Annual plans must include concrete descriptions of how you intend to accomplish such objectives—for example, growing the parents fund through the recruitment of 20 volunteer peer solicitors and 60 to 75 personal solicitations.
- *Dates.* Here's where planning differences between individuals may be most apparent. Some teams prefer to have every date of every project clearly defined, while others simply indicate the actual "launch" date of a project, and allow the details to flow from there. Regardless, the key is to know when a project has to launch to be effective in the fund-raising year.
- *Quantitative and qualitative targets.* Again, "grow the parents fund" is certainly an objective, but you must specify an amount if you expect to evaluate your year. Without a specific target, you might consider growth of $1,000 a success, but what if you invested nearly $40,000 in that growth through the addition of programs and staff? Alternatively, suppose you set a target of growing the parents fund by $100,000 and achieved that, but you did not recruit any parents to help as volunteers. In this case,

you hit the quantitative target, but failed to recognize—and achieve—a qualitative one. Defining both types of targets is important in sustaining programs over the long term.

This regular planning process is a mandatory step every year. Without it, you have no sense of direction or goals, and no real answer to the question, "So, how's the year going?" With it, you have the confidence of knowing when your efforts are working and when they are not. You can also evaluate your progress throughout the year so you can turn to backup options when a solicitation doesn't go as smoothly as you'd hoped.

Real-Life Points for Practice

Schedule time twice a year (or even quarterly or monthly) to formally report your results to someone—your boss, staff, volunteers, peers, etc. It will help you better understand your program by organizing a presentation and answering questions. Furthermore, it will raise the profile of the annual fund among your listeners.

GROWTH PLANNING

Periodically, you will have reason to go through the more comprehensive type of planning that, for the purposes of this book, we are calling "growth planning." The process is typically prompted by an outside force such as a campaign, a new CEO, a change in the alumni relationship to the institution, or a crisis.

Growth planning does not necessarily have clear start and end points. It doesn't fall into a neat set of five or 10 steps, and it doesn't fit nicely into a 12- to 18-month window. It can take anywhere from a month to two years or more. It may involve an in-depth analysis of your own numbers, as well as an exhaustive review of peer programs. Often, it requires the expertise of an outside evaluator, such as a consultant or peer reviewer, who can come in without history or institutional "baggage," study your program, and make specific recommendations.

Following are some general paths through which growth plans develop and ways you might respond to these situations.

Poor performance in one or more crucial areas of annual giving. Every program, no matter how successful, can identify an area that is not reaching its optimal level. In this case, however, we're talking about a program that is significantly deficient in one or more key areas.

For example, let's say you manage a program that consistently hits or comes close to your revenue projections. You lead your peer group in alumni participation and consistently grow your leadership donor revenue by 10 to 15 percent. However, a campaign consultant (or a new boss) pushes for additional analysis in preparation for an upcoming campaign feasibility study. After thorough examination, you determine that your LYBUNT retention (the rate by which you retain donors from one fiscal year to the next) has hovered around 45 percent for the last three years. Although your other performance figures are strong, this is an area of significant vulnerability. The implication, obviously, is that you do not have a core set of donors who support you year after year. Instead, you're relying on the significant acquisition of donors from individuals who either haven't given in the past or whose giving has lapsed. While that's a strength in itself, your program has tremendous growth opportunity if you can identify a way to raise your LYBUNT retention to 70 or even 80 percent.

Typically, problems like this are not easily fixed by just sending one more piece of direct mail or one more phonathon pledge reminder. You now have an opportunity to identify your problem and create solutions by steps such as these:

- *Obtaining more data.* Will a focus group or donor survey help you identify causes for your problem? Does your database reveal any attribute that connects the constituents you're focusing on (i.e., are they typically younger or older donors, etc.)?
- *Checking with peer programs.* Have any of your peers successfully addressed this problem? Can you steal/borrow program ideas?
- *Determining growth potential and resource allocation.* What is the financial value of these lost donors? How much are you, therefore, willing to spend to strengthen your program?

From these and other steps, you can identify a course of action, develop a strong case for your solution, seek funding, integrate this new effort with your current program, and launch your solution.

A "life change" in your institution. Life changes can range from the arrival of a new CEO to the launch of a comprehensive campaign to the celebration of a centennial. Such life changes provide an opportunity to strengthen your annual giving program. In many cases, the desire for improvement isn't necessarily precipitated by the need to fix an underperforming program. Instead, the life event encourages you to explore any and all areas of growth. Furthermore, the annual giving program may provide the chance to involve even more of your constituents in the institutional life event.

For example, if your institution were about to celebrate the 100th anniversary of its founding, undoubtedly various components will plan a broad array of activities, programs, and fund-raising initiatives to help commemorate the event. If your annual fund is well managed and performs consistently each year with 5 percent growth in both revenue and donors, there may not be a readily apparent area for improvement. However, with further discussion, you may determine that now is a good time to push for a particularly aggressive goal of 1,900 members in your President's Club (current membership just over 1,000). By any measure, this represents a significant growth of 90 percent in one year. In this situation, you might proceed with your growth plan by

- *Assessing your current staff and resource allocation.* Are there areas you can pull back from in order to redeploy resources in pursuit of this goal? Will you need additional funding?
- *Researching other programs that may have achieved this growth.* Again, there may be opportunities to steal or borrow ideas.
- *Setting very careful benchmarks.* In light of the ambitious goal, you should identify points during the year at which you can take the pulse of the effort. Are you at your halfway mark when you predicted? Will you reach your goal with the number of visits or mailings still on the calendar?
- *Including post-growth issues in your plans.* If your influx of staff and resources is temporary, how will you maintain this new level? Have you planned proper stewardship of your new donors to ensure a high rate of renewal? If you pull back on another program during the centennial year, how will you address any repercussions in the following year?

A change in your staffing. Another opportunity for growth planning is afforded not necessarily by design, but by circumstance. As most managers do not have the flexibility to add staff on a regular basis, attrition provides an opportunity to examine your program and either reaffirm or change your staffing configuration.

For example, your program may have two individuals running the phone and mail efforts, leaving the director to manage all volunteers, parents, and high-end personal solicitations. If one of your two phone/mail staff members leaves for another opportunity, you now have a flexible resource to evaluate. Perhaps you've always felt that having another person "on the road" with you would make a significant difference in your revenue from high-end annual fund donors. With the departure of one staff member, you now have the option of consolidating responsibilities into the remaining position. For example, by adding a part-time student worker to handle some of the tasks, or by outsourcing a portion of the direct mail (with some additional budget) you can hire a senior staffer to join you in personal solicitation. This is an oversimplified example, but it illustrates how you can respond creatively when presented with the flexible resource of an open personnel line.

In summary, growth planning comprises the extraordinary efforts involved in making significant changes to a program in pursuit of extraordinary growth in revenue or donors. The planning you do consists of the annual adjustments you make to your existing program in order to maintain the growth level you expect annually. The two are not mutually exclusive and all good managers are thinking of both simultaneously. One of the most important questions an annual giving officer can address is, "Where would you spend an additional $100,000 in budget?" The dollar figure isn't particularly relevant other than it should be significant enough to make a difference. What is more important is your awareness of where growth opportunities lie within your program.

Chapter 18

Evaluation and Benchmarking

IT WAS HARD TO DECIDE WHETHER THE CHAPTER ON PLANNING should precede the chapter on evaluation, or vice versa. Intuition would suggest that you would need to have planned something—and executed it—before it can be evaluated. But as you have probably recognized, much of the planning process is based on evaluation of the prior year(s). In the simplest terms, evaluation is the process of lining up your goals and objectives in one column and your corresponding results in another, and circling the areas where you exceeded your goal in green, for example, and the areas where you missed your goal in red.

Most programs, though, are far too complex to stop with a simple, two-column approach. Evaluation involves a numerical comparison, a programmatic comparison, and an overall review of program strategy and resources. The evaluation process must occur at the end of each year, but it is also appropriate to evaluate periodically throughout the year to allow yourself the opportunity to make quick adjustments if a program is under performing. Evaluation should involve multiple individuals, not just the annual giving director. Seek input from colleagues, volunteers, supervisors, and staff.

Beyond just the comparison from one column to the next, successful evaluations must include all of the following components.

A quantitative analysis of all of your solicitation efforts from the year. This ties back to the planning discussion, because an analysis doesn't simply imply a straight numbers comparison. It involves exploring those results that either exceeded or missed your goal, and identifying why.

Again, there's nearly always a statistical "driver" that will help you answer that question. If your phonathon missed its goal of $2 million in pledges, you can find the answer in your telemarketing statistics. It may have been a lower-than-expected pledge rate, fulfillment rate, or average pledge. Regardless, as you line up your columns of goals and results, you should be able to identify the "why" for almost all of them. Almost all, because occasionally you will encounter a program or a solicitation effort that has all of the key indicators for success, but falls completely flat without a readily apparent reason.

The key to this quantitative analysis is to identify the "why" of performance issues in a way that will enable you to make decisions about next year. Let's go back to our phonathon example. Let's say you have missed your goal of $2 million in pledges and you determine that the problem is the increasing number of incorrect telephone numbers in your database. You can develop a strategy for the year ahead in which you aggressively pursue phone number research and database clean-up.

A qualitative review of your program efforts. Without downplaying the importance of the quantitative analysis, another important evaluative step is to review your program efforts for quality and reach (as in, "How many people were affected by this program?"). Although annual giving is an enterprise driven by numbers, it is equally important to sustain efforts that cannot necessarily be quantified. For example, efforts involving matching gift agent volunteers may not necessarily increase overall revenue from corporate match programs, but they do create an entry-level position for volunteers. It also may help to strengthen relationships with several key corporations—a step that may, in turn, lead to larger corporate opportunities including philanthropy, job recruiting, and more. These types of qualitative observations would override the suggestion of discarding the program, given the less than impressive quantitative results.

A review of budget and personnel allocation. Although this factor doesn't fit neatly into a column next to performance numbers, it's important to evaluate your resource allocation in the office and make adjustments when needed. As you review your performance figures, consider whether there are places where efforts among staff can be consolidated, or budget dollars can be redirected to allow for more solicitations. Has a program matured to a stage where less staff time is required and you can use the surplus staff to explore a new opportunity? (I imagine that many readers may chuckle at the notion of "surplus staff." Instead, consider your "surplus time.")

Support of the overall development effort. As we have discussed, one of the key functions of the annual fund is to help identify major gift donors. While this may not be a task you can set numerical targets for, it should be a part of your evaluation. This is particularly important as you attempt to create internal support for your efforts.

An opportunity to share your evaluation. Your year-end program evaluation should not sit on a shelf. Seek opportunities to present, distribute, and discuss your findings. Create partnerships with colleagues as you search for ways to improve. Most important, raise the awareness of others at your institution by demonstrating the positive impact of the annual fund.

The chapter on planning made several references to benchmarking and comparing your program with that of a peer institution. Do not underestimate the importance of this; you have little way to gauge your potential other than comparing your efforts to those of your peers. Although the experiences at no two institutions are the same, there are many similarities you can draw on when exploring new programs, strengthening existing ones, or changing strategies. The best strategy is to develop an amalgam of peer programs that you can make comparisons to and borrow ideas from.

There is a wide array of items you can benchmark with a peer program. The most popular include

- total dollars raised;
- alumni participation rate;
- alumni of record;
- giving from other constituents (friends, parents, faculty/staff);
- budget size and allocation;
- attendance at reunions or other events;
- phonathon pledges, pledge rates, and other telemarketing details; and
- direct mail response rates, costs, etc.

However, beyond these staples of comparison are a host of other details that will help you develop strategies and evaluate your efforts more thoroughly. Some include

- staffing structure and responsibilities;
- staff reward systems (financial and nonfinancial);
- volunteer recruitment and training programs;
- specific strategies with segments (young alumni, theater patrons, etc.); and
- donor retention rates and strategies.

The list could continue for several pages, but this covers many of the basics. The value of collecting this information is that it provides you with both a sense of your relative success, and the ability to make assumptions about the growth opportunities in your program.

If XYZ College spends an additional $35,000 on the phonathon pledge reminder process, and has a 25 percent higher donor retention than your efforts produce, what does that say? First, it doesn't say you can invest $35,000 and expect the same result. It does, however, indicate that there may be a correlation between the college's increased investment in this area and its additional revenue. The key is to determine whether there are other variables that may contribute to the difference that would neutralize the budget comparison. For example, if this peer institution awards some type of preferential system for buying athletic tickets that includes gift renewal as a variable, then it's quite likely that the tickets, and not the additional $35,000, are driving the high donor retention. This example is fairly obvious, but as you compare and benchmark your program, there may be other variables that are not so obvious and require a thorough exploration before you make assumptions about adopting the strategy of a peer.

There are multiple ways to get the data by which you can benchmark, including

- published reports, such as the annual *Voluntary Support of Education* published by Council for Aid to Education (CAE) and various CASE publications, such as the Annual *CASE Report of Educational Fund-Raising Campaigns*;
- e-mail listservs such as Fundlist, an online forum for people who

are mostly entry- to mid-level fund raisers, people who work on the annual fund, people in advancement services, and a few consultants and vendors;

- written surveys to your counterparts at peer institutions;
- telephone surveys of your counterparts; and
- on-site visits to peer institutions.

These are listed in order of the intrusiveness on your peer institution, lowest to highest. They are also listed in order of effectiveness for securing beneficial information that can help you plan. One wonderful thing about the development profession is our willingness to share details and ideas with one another. At the same time, recognize the significant effort you may require of a peer who has agreed to provide you with the information, and be judicious in your inquiries.

Real-Life Points for Practice

Consider recruiting a network of four to six professionals from peer institutions. Coordinate times throughout the year to participate in conference calls, in-person meetings, or simply e-mail exchanges. Develop a chart of statistics that you can share between your respective programs, and refresh that chart periodically during the fiscal year.

Closing Thoughts

If you have been compulsive enough to read this book from cover to cover in one sitting, your head must be spinning. Very few parts of the development process have as many facets to explore as annual giving, and we did not address them all.

To close with the right tone, I'll restate my goal from the beginning. This approach to a comprehensive guide should be extremely helpful for individuals with little experience in annual giving. While it is not a step-by-step guide on "how to run a phonathon," it should provide an overview that will enable you to better understand articles and books on phonathons, and empower you to create your own guide. And while you won't find the top 10 ways to recruit callers, you will learn the importance of a solid recruiting effort, and how to explore and identify your own "top 10."

In addition, this guide should help people who have significant experience in the annual fund. While you may not need to think through the reasons why you send direct mail, you may benefit from the opportunity to recenter your thinking on direct mail, and a host of other subjects. It is easy to get consumed with the day-to-day operations and numbers, and lose sight of the need to pull back and carefully evaluate where the program is today and where it's headed tomorrow. The discipline of annual giving requires an approach that balances short-term activities with a long-term focus. The successful practitioners are those who can maintain that balance.

As you have probably noticed, most of the chapters in this book contained some type of list—ways to include annual giving in a campaign, reasons for direct mail, components of a successful plan, etc. In keeping with that theme, I'll close with a list of "take-home" ideas. No matter what you may remember about specific tools or programs, try to carry away the following ideas from this book:

- *Be a catalyst at your organization.* While you may not always have the authority to make every decision, you do have the information to help others make the right decisions. Think about ways in which you can inform decision makers about numbers and trends so that the annual fund is a key component in overall development strategy.
- *Make a commitment.* Real progress in an annual giving program happens over time. Of course, as an annual fund officer, you may be able to make changes that immediately improve the bottom line. However, long-term, strategic growth occurs over time, and requires a commitment from the staff and volunteers to lead that growth.
- *Develop your network.* With few exceptions, there may be no one else at your organization who does exactly what you do. However, there's a good chance that someone at an organization across town or in another region does have similar responsibilities. Get to know that person, because you will be invaluable resources to each other as you both grow your programs.
- *Never lose sight of the individual donor.* As much as annual giving is about numbers, it is also about individuals. If we adopt the stance that there's always another nondonor to take a donor's place, we may soon find ourselves in the position of having nothing but nondonors to work with.
- *Explore your own thoughts and ideas.* This book is just a compilation of thoughts, ideas, and observations. You may agree with all of them, or only a few. In fact, you may strongly disagree with many of them, and that's good. Unlike professionals in a field like accounting, we have no set-in-stone rules to govern our instincts. No one can absolutely tell you that idea "A" will raise more money than idea "B" until you test it. Push your own envelope, and think about why things happen and what you can do to grow your program.

Best wishes for your success in annual giving, or wherever you may find yourself.

Useful Terms

Below are some terms that commonly arise in annual giving operations. Not all of these terms appear in this book; the definitions here should give you enough information to understand them as you hear them used in practice and when you read them in the context of more detailed articles and how-to books on annual giving programs. Italics indicate words that are defined elsewhere in this list.

Acquisition: as a verb, the process of acquiring donors from your *non-donor* or *never-giver* ranks. As a noun, the term can refer collectively to nondonors and never-givers, as in "We'll send this letter to *LYBUNTs* and *SYBUNTs*, and that letter to Acquisition."

Appeal tracking code (also *solicit code* or **appeal code**)**:** a unique alphanumeric code assigned to individual segments within phone and mail solicitations. These codes allow for the tracking of revenue produced by these solicitations, as well as for comparisons and analysis of the resulting data.

Automated phonathon: a phonathon program that uses computers and specialized software to assist in making calls. Some vendors of these services use the labels "automated" and "predictive" to distinguish between programs that simply automate the dialing process, and enhanced programs that use a *predictive dialing* system to place a larger volume of calls.

BRE: business reply envelope. See *reply envelope.*

Completion rate (also *penetration rate*)**:** the portion of a pool of prospects that was actually contacted in some meaningful way. The term is usually applied to phonathon programs. For example, if you have a telemarketing segment of 1,000 prospects, and for 825, you made contact or had some other terminating result (such as deceased, already gave, changed address, etc.), then you reached an 82.5 percent completion rate. It is rare to see completion rates above 90 percent because of such factors as unanswered calls, answering machines, caller ID, and wrong numbers. Compare with *fulfillment rate*; *yield rate.*

Conversion rate: most commonly, the percentage of *nondonors* converted to donors in a given year. For example, "Our conversion rate this year was 23 percent" implies that 23 percent of all nondonors made a gift during this fiscal year. Compare with *participation rate*; *retention rate*; *SYBUNTs*.

Cost-per-dollar-raised (also **cost-to-raise-a-dollar**)**:** a gauge of efficiency and effectiveness that calculates the cost of each dollar raised. To calculate this, you divide the cost of a program by the resulting gift income. For example, if you spend $5,000 on a mailing (including postage, printing, and so forth) and the mailing raised $35,000, then the cost-per-dollar-raised was 14.3 cents. Keep in mind that younger programs are more expensive, particularly those that seek to acquire donors from largely nondonor populations. Overall average for an annual giving program should range between 10 cents to 50 cents. Some annual giving professionals have said that if you are not spending at least 25 cents on the dollar, then you're not spending enough.

CRE: courtesy reply envelope. See *reply envelope.*

Dollars-per-decision: a gauge of efficiency and effectiveness for phonathons that measures how much your program raises with every decision (yes or no) made on the phone. Compare with *cost-per-dollar-raised.*

Dual ask (also **double ask**): the process whereby major gift donors are solicited for both an annual, current-use gift and a major capital or endowment gift.

EFT: electronic funds transfer, a relatively new method (introduced in the 1990s) by which donors may make contributions. Typically, a donor determines a monthly gift amount and then authorizes your organization to directly debit his or her bank account. The funds are transferred electronically to your institution.

Fulfillment rate: the percentage of pledges, typically from phonathons, that donors fulfill. Fulfillment statistics may also track the dollar amount of pledges and the number of individual pledges. Between 75 to 95 percent is considered an acceptable range for pledge fulfillment, as almost all programs anticipate some default on pledges. Compare with *completion rate; yield rate.*

LYBUNT: an acronym for a donor who gave Last Year But Unfortunately Not This year. If it's fiscal year 2001, *LYBUNTs* are donors from fiscal year 2000 who have not yet renewed their gifts.

Matching gift: a contribution received from a corporation in response to a contribution made by one of its employees. There are more than 7,000 matching gift companies, each of which develops its own rules regarding the size of the gift, acceptable recipients, frequency of gifts, and other criteria.

NCOA: National Change of Address, a service that enables you to compare your database with the national postal service listing of address changes filed by individuals when they move. To qualify for some postal rates, you must have passed your address file through this process within a recent time period.

Never-giver: a donor prospect who has never given a gift. This term is typically used by institutions that define *nondonor* as a past donor whose most recent gift was too long ago to qualify as a *SYBUNT.*

Nondonor: depending on your program, either (1) someone who has never made a gift, or (2) a donor whose most recent gift was made earlier than a specific date range. See *SYBUNT; never-giver.*

Participation rate: the number of donors divided by the number of addressable prospects. The term is usually applied to alumni, e.g. "We reached 25 percent alumni participation this year." It may also be used with other donor populations, such as parents, patients, friends, faculty/staff, etc. Compare with *conversion rate; retention rate.*

Penetration rate: see *completion rate.*

Predictive dialing: an enhancement to an *automated phonathon* system that uses a central dialer mechanism to make calls and relay any "live" connections to a waiting telemarketer. The dialer uses more outbound lines than there are telemarketers, so it must "predict" how quickly to place these calls to ensure that a telemarketer will be available to take over successful connections.

Prospect management system (also *tracking system*)**:** any system that assists development staff in managing, tracking, and planning communication and activity involving donors and potential donors. While this may involve computer software, it also may be as simple as written journals and "tickler" files. A management system should provide both a repository of history and detail of contacts with individuals as well as a proactive planning mechanism for future activities.

Quid pro quo: a Latin phrase that, loosely translated, means "this for that." In an annual giving context, the term refers to gifts to your organization that involve some type of benefit to the donor, thereby affecting the tax deductibility of the gift.

Reply envelope: an envelope sent with solicitations to facilitate the return of contributions. A reply envelope is sometimes called a #9 envelope, referring to its standard size, which fits inside a standard #10 or business-sized envelope. A *CRE* (courtesy reply envelope) requires the donor to affix a stamp. On a *BRE* (business reply envelope), return postage is prepaid by the organization.

Response rate: see *yield rate.*

Retention rate: the number of last year's givers who give again this year. For example, if you had 10,000 donors last year and 7,600 renewed their gifts this year, then your donor retention rate is 76 percent. A range of 60 to 80 percent retention is considered average. Compare with *conversion rate; participation rate.*

Solicit code: see *appeal tracking code.*

SYBUNT: an acronym for a donor who gave Some Year(s) But Unfortunately Not This year. The "some" year(s) can be defined in a variety of ways, but typically ranges from two to seven years preceding the current year. For example, if it's fiscal year 2001, a SYBUNT may have given in fiscal year 1996, with no gift since.

Tracking system: see *prospect management system.*

Yield rate (also *response rate*)**:** a measure typically used with direct mail to describe the percentage of recipients who respond to a mailing. Yield rates can range from 1 to 2 percent on certain *nondonor* mailings to as high as 50 to 75 percent for mailings to donors and leadership groups. Compare with *completion rate; fulfillment rate.*

Additional Resources

ANNUAL GIVING

Beattie, Kathleen M. "Listen to Employees!: By Rethinking the Way it Conducted its Employee Giving Campaigns, Orlando Regional Healthcare Foundation Developed a Strong Case for Annual Support," *Fund Raising Management* 26, no. 9 (November 1995): 14-17.

Bragg, Bob. "Seven Ideas for Highly Effective Fund Raising: To Achieve the Best Results from All Your Callers, Regardless of Their Skills, You Must Have an Effective Training Program and Motivational Reward System," *Fund Raising Management* 28, no. 2 (April 1997): 14-15.

Britz, Jennifer Delahunty. "Promises to Keep: After the Annual Fund Proposal, Encourage Alumni to Fulfill Their Pledge to Alma Mater," CURRENTS 22, no. 7 (July/August 1996): 34-

Caldwell, Robert M. "Closing the Year Successfully: How to Evaluate Your Annual Fund Program," In *Classic Currents: Annual Giving: 14 Articles on Planning, Mail and Phone Solicitations, Closing the Year Successfully, Tips from the Experts, and More.* Compiled by Lindy Keane Carter. Washington, DC: Council for Advancement and Support of Education, 1998. 54-57.

Carney, Joe. "Defending Our Honor: We Need to Convince Our Alumni that Student Callers Aren't Telemarketers. The Difference? Students Care About Our Cause," CURRENTS 20, no. 8 (September 1994): 64.

Ciconte, Barbara, and Jeanne G. Jacob. *Fund Raising Basics: A Complete Guide.* Frederick, MD: Aspen Publishers, February 1997. 315 pages.

Colson, Helen A. *Philanthropy at Independent Schools.* Washington, DC: National Association of Independent Schools, 1996. 105 pages.

Goodale, Toni K. "Consultant's Corner: Maintaining the Annual Fund," *Fund Raising Management* 27, no. 1 (March 1996): 54-55.

Greenfield, James M. *Fund Raising Fundamentals: A Guide to Annual Giving for Professionals and Volunteers.* New York, NY: John Wiley and Sons Inc., 1994. 407 pages.

Grizzard, Claude T. Jr. "The 10 Basic Commandments of Successful Fund Raising: This Checklist Contains the Ingredients Necessary for a Smooth, Record-Shattering Campaign. Each of These Commandments Must Be Clearly Apparent—And Followed to Insure a Successful Effort," *Fund Raising Management* 27, no. 5 (July 1996): 26-30.

Hauk, Jeff, and Robert A. Burdenski. "Great Catches: Fish Through Your Database for New Annual Fund Prospect Segments," CURRENTS 25, no. 4 (April 1999): 24-28.

Hummerstone, Robert G. "World-Class Annual Funds: Here's How to Take Your Appeal Abroad to Tap Some of Your Best Prospects," CURRENTS 24, no. 4 (April 1998): 40-45.

"Independent Girls' Schools Fare Best in Annual Giving," *Fund Raising Management* 29, no. 2 (April 1998): 13.

Jackson, Laura Christion. "Concentrated Efforts: For Alumni Offices that Don't Manage Annual Giving, the Focus Is on Friend Raising, Not Fund Raising," CURRENTS 23, no. 5 (May 1997): 14.

Keller, Thomas K. "Lamentations and Letter Writing," *Fund Raising Management* 27, no. 12 (February 1997): 24-27.

Kelly, Kathleen S. *Effective Fund-Raising Management.* Hillsdale, NJ: Lawrence Erlbaum Associates, 1998. 663 pages.

Klein, Kim. *Fund Raising for Social Change*. 3rd ed. Berkeley, CA: Chardon Press, 1995. 351 pages.

Lansdowne, David. *The Relentlessly Practical Guide to Raising Serious Money: Proven Strategies for Nonprofit Organizations*. Medfield, MA: Emerson and Church, January 1997. 264 pages.

"The Latest from the Listservs: Creative Comebacks to Phonathon Pitches," CURRENTS 22, no. 9 (October 1996): 7.

Lysakowski, Linda, and Judith Snyder. "Fund Raising on Main Street: Local Business Support of Your Annual Fund Can Solidify Your Campus's Ties to its Community," CURRENTS 26, no. 1 (January 2000): 34-37.

Muro, James J. *Creating and Funding Educational Foundations: A Guide for Local School Districts*. Boston, MA: Allyn and Bacon, 1995.

National Society of Fund Raising Executives. *1996 Conference Proceedings: A Compilation of Educational Session Reference Materials*. Alexandria, VA: National Society of Fund Raising Executives, 1996. 518 pages.

O'Shea, Catherine L. "Fasten Your Seatbelts: When Your Campaign Encounters Turbulence, Try These Tips for Riding Out the Bumps," CURRENTS 26, no. 1 (January 2000): 13.

Squires, Con. "Using Skillful Direct Mail Methods Towards Your Fund Raising Efforts," *Fund Raising Management* 28, no. 1 (March 1997): 36-37.

Taylor, Amy Jo. "Big Things from Small Packages: How to Motivate Student Callers in Tight Places on a Tight Budget," CURRENTS 24, no. 5 (May 1998): 64.

Walker, Mary Margaret. "Balancing Act: Managing Alumni Relations and the Annual Fund Is No Easy Feat. To Master the Art, Begin with These Five Lessons," CURRENTS 23, no. 5 (May 1997): 10-14.

Woolbright, Cynthia, and Heather Calvin. "The Strategic Annual Fund: How Smith College Overhauled its Efforts, Assumptions, and Goals—And Set Fund-Raising Success in Motion," CURRENTS 22, no. 8 (September 1996): 45-49.

ANNUAL GIVING: BUILDING PARTICIPATION IN THE ANNUAL FUND

Beattie, Kathleen M. "Listen to Employees!: By Rethinking the Way it Conducted its Employee Giving Campaigns, Orlando Regional Healthcare Foundation Developed a Strong Case for Annual Support," *Fund Raising Management* 26, no. 9 (November 1995): 14-17.

Britz, Jennifer Delahunty. "Promises to Keep: After the Annual Fund Proposal, Encourage Alumni to Fulfill Their Pledge to Alma Mater," CURRENTS 22, no. 7 (July/August 1996): 34-

"Dealing with Objections: For Every Reason Not to Give, There's a More Compelling Reason to Give. Here's How to Turn Common Donor Objections into Stronger Cases for Support," CURRENTS 23, no. 4 (April 1997): 28-33.

"Expert Advice: Consultants Tell How to Handle Several Campaign Conundrums," CURRENTS 21, no. 10 (November/December 1995): 72-

Grizzard, Claude T. Jr. "The 10 Basic Commandments of Successful Fund Raising: This Checklist Contains the Ingredients Necessary for a Smooth, Record-Shattering Campaign. Each of These Commandments Must Be Clearly Apparent—And Followed to Insure a Successful Effort," *Fund Raising Management* 27, no. 5 (July 1996): 26-30.

Hauk, Jeff, and Robert A. Burdenski. "Great Catches: Fish Through Your Database for New Annual Fund Prospect Segments," CURRENTS 25, no. 4 (April 1999): 24-28.

Heuermann, Robert. "A Higher Calling: Your Fund-Raising Efforts Are Crucial to the Future. Here's Why," CURRENTS 23, no. 4 (April 1997): 16-18.

Hummerstone, Robert G. "World-Class Annual Funds: Here's How to Take Your Appeal Abroad to Tap Some of Your Best Prospects," CURRENTS 24, no. 4 (April 1998): 40-45.

Jackson, Laura Christion. "Concentrated Efforts: For Alumni Offices That Don't Manage Annual Giving, the Focus Is on Friend Raising, Not Fund Raising," CURRENTS 23, no. 5 (May 1997): 14.

Pollack, Rachel H. "Divide and Conquer: Get More from Your Annual Fund by Targeting Appeals to Special Groups," CURRENTS 24, no. 5 (May 1998): 12-19.

Williams, Karla A. *Donor Focused Strategies for Annual Giving.* Gaithersburg, MD: Aspen Publishers, July 1997. 287 pages.

Woolbright, Cynthia. "Closing the Year Successfully: Planning for a Successful Annual Fund: Key Components of an Effective Program," In *Classic Currents: Annual Giving: 14 Articles on Planning, Mail and Phone Solicitations, Closing the Year Successfully, Tips from the Experts, and More.* Washington, DC: Council for Advancement and Support of Education, 1998. 2-5.

Wylie, Peter B. "Model Behavior: Statistical Modeling Can Help You Find the Right Equation for Annual Fund Success," CURRENTS 25, no. 4 (April 1999): 16-23.

ANNUAL FUND: DIRECT MAIL STRATEGIES

Armstrong, Richard. "The Route to Effective Fund-Raising Letters: Not-For-Profits Should Take a Lesson from Commercial Marketers, the Author Argues. The Goal of Direct Mail Is to Convince People Who

Already Agrée with You that Your Organization Is the Best Route to Achieving Their Goal," *Advancing Philanthropy* 3, no. 3 (Fall 1995): 42-43.

Christ, Rick. "Put Your Direct Mail to the Test: Try Out New Annual-Fund Strategies—One at a Time—To Increase Your Returns with Less Risk," CURRENTS 24, no. 5 (May 1998): 20-24, 26.

Craver, Roger M. "Get Ready for Tomorrow!: While Old-Style Direct Mail Is Dead, an Exciting New Form of Direct Response Is Rising to Take its Place. New Technologies Provide Access to More People on an Individualized Basis," *Fund Raising Management* 25, no. 11 (January 1995): 26-29.

Gafke, Roger. "Correspondence Course: Ten Steps to Make Your Annual Fund Letter a Winner from Planning to Postscript," CURRENTS 22, no. 5 (May 1996): 18-

Hamilton, Gail. *Fundraiser's Phrase Book*. Toronto, ON: Hamilton House, 1996. 522 pages.

Hauk, Jeff. "Is Direct Mail Dead? Although Use May Be Waning, Direct Mail Is Still a Viable Fund-Raising Format. Here Are 10 Ways Campuses Are Breathing New Life into the Medium," CURRENTS 24, no. 9 (October 1998): 44-51.

Huntsinger, Jerry. "Direct Mail Fund Raising in the Year 2001: In 2001 Direct-Mail Fund Raisers Will Have Learned to Live with a Low Percent of Response and a High Average Gift. Mailing Lists Will Be Smarter but More Dynamic," *Fund Raising Management* 25, no. 1 (March 1994): 32-

Huntsinger, Jerry. "How to Write Letters to 'Old People': Don't Make the Mistake of Lumping All Seniors into One Super Category. There Are Really Three Categories—and Knowing How to Approach Each One Can Make a Big Difference in Your Direct Mail Fund Raising," *Fund Raising Management* 25, no. 11 (January 1995): 34-37.

Jardine, Fred, and Don Schoenleber. "And the Winner Is...Premiums and Incentives Have Long Been Used in Fund-Raising Direct Mail. Here's a Look at What Works and What Fails—And How to Make What Works Work Better—From Two Long-Term Experts in Creative Direct-Mail Formats," *Fund Raising Management* 29, no. 2 (April 1998): 20-22.

Kitcatt, Paul, and Joe Saxton. "Are Your Appeals the Brussels Sprouts of Fund Raising? For too Many Organizations the Process of Creating a Direct Mail Appeal Has Become Cumbersome, Mechanical and Uninspiring. Here's a Way to Prevent That," *Fund Raising Management* 24, no. 11 (January 1994): 29-

Lewis, Herschell Gordon. "Does Your Envelope Plead, Scream or Demand?: Testing, to Prove that Your Envelope Treatment Hasn't Inadvertently Alienated Prospects Instead of Attracting Them, Will Give You Useful Marketing Information," *Fund Raising Management* 25, no. 11 (January 1995): 17-19.

Lewis, Herschell Gordon. "Direct Mail Fund Raising Tactics: Sooner or Later Most Direct Marketers Are Involved in Fund Raising Campaigns. Fund Raisers Are in the Vanguard of Direct Marketing Because Theirs Is One of the Most Competitive Situations. Techniques that Worked Ten Years Ago Now Are Overworked. What Does Bring Response Today?" *Fund Raising Management* 28, no. 5 (July 1997): 17-19.

Mandel, Leslie. "100% Delivered: The Goal of the Direct Mail Industry. The Prayer of the Mailer. The Hope of the Post Office," *Fund Raising Management* 26, no. 11 (January 1996): 16-19.

McNamee, Mike. "Dealing with Donor Anger: Sure, the Public Is Mad About Junk Mail and Junk Calls. But Campus Fund Raisers Don't Have to Worry About Hostile Alumni—Or Do They?," CURRENTS 21, no. 4 (April 1995): 16-21.

Ouellette, John. "Helping Volunteers Write a Successful Fund Raising Letter," *Ensemble* 7, no. 1 (Spring 1997): 12.

Printz, Jenny, and Dwight Maltby. "Beyond Personalization: When Handwriting Makes a Difference," *Fund Raising Management* 28, no. 3 (May 1997): 16-19.

Rieck, Dean. "Powerful Fund-Raising Letters—From A to Z: Part One of Three; Despite All the New Technology and Media We Have Available Today, the Letter Remains One of the Best Ways to Solicit Funds from a Wide Audience. It's Personal, Direct, and Cost-Effective," *Fund Raising Management* 29, no. 2 (April 1998): 25-28.

Rieck, Dean. "Powerful Fund-Raising Letters—From A to Z: Part Three of Three," *Fund Raising Management* 29, no. 4 (June 1998): 31-33.

Rieck, Dean. "Powerful Fund-Raising Letters—From A to Z: Part Two of Three," *Fund Raising Management* 29, no. 3 (May 1998): 28-30.

Rosen, Lou. "The Core of a Successful Fund-Raising System: If Your Direct-Mail System Does Not Contain the Necessary Features to Segment and Report Mailing Results for Analysis, You're Certain to Be Missing Out on a Potential Net Income," *Fund Raising Management* 25, no. 11 (January 1995): 14-16.

Ryan, Ellen. "Annual Fund Answers: Experts in Direct Mail, Phonathons, and In-Person Asks Tackle Some of the Annual Fund's Perennial Problems," CURRENTS 22, no. 5 (May 1996): 30-

Ryan, Ellen. "An Annual Swap Fest: Tips, Advice, and Ideas to Boost Your Fund-Raising Success—From Colleges Around the Continent," CURRENTS 21, no. 4 (April 1995): 10-12, 14.

Squires, Con. "Recapturing the Lapsed Perennial Donor, Part I," *Fund Raising Management* 28, no. 7 (September 1997): 32-33.

Squires, Con. "Recapturing the Lapsed Perennial Donor, Part II," *Fund Raising Management* 28, no. 8 (October 1997): 36-37.

"Stamps May Boost Direct Mail Response," *Fund Raising Management* 27, no. 12 (February 1997): 11.

Warwick, Mal. *Raising Money by Mail: Strategies for Growth and Financial Stability.* Berkeley, CA: Strathmoor Press, March 1996. 128 pages.

ANNUAL GIVING: DONOR RECOGNITION, GIFT CLUBS, AND CHALLENGE GIFTS

Borenstein, Henry P. "Recognition: The Stepchild of Fundraising: In Creating Donor Recognition Programs, There Are Several Points to Consider Along with Some Areas of Concern," *Fund Raising Management* 23, no. 2 (April 1992): 18-

Collins, Mary Ellen. "Noteworthy Thank-Yous: Don't Let Acknowledgment Anxiety Cramp Your Letter-Writing Style," CURRENTS 25, no. 5 (May 1999): 16.

Collins, Walton R. "The Subtleties: Some Fund Raisers Regard Stewardship Only as a Buzz Word. Others Define the Concept Narrowly, as Finding Ways to Say 'Thank You' for Gifts. At its Most Effective, Though, Stewardship is the Focused Application of Recognition," *Advancing Philanthropy*, no. 4 (Fall 1996): 12-16.

Dessoff, Alan L. "Put it in Writing: Don't Let Donor Thanks Fall by the Wayside. Create a Written Recognition Policy to Make Thank-Yous a Part of Your Development Office Routine," CURRENTS 23, no. 2 (February 1997): 30-34.

Donor Relations: The Essential Guide to Stewardship Policies, Procedures, and Protocol. Washington, DC: Council for Advancement and Support of Education, 1998. 97 pages.

Ensman, Richard G. Jr. "Synchronicity: A New Name for an Old Idea," *Fund Raising Management* 28, no. 4 (June 1997): 18-19.

Ensman, Richard G. Jr. "Turn 'Small Shops' into 'Big Shops' Via the Internet," *Fund Raising Management* 26, no. 2 (April 1995): 28-29.

Harrison, Bill. "When a Plaque Isn't Enough: How Do You Thank Major Donors? Planning What to Do After Receipt of a Gift Begins Long Before the Actual Event. Recognition of Major Donors Is One of the Most Important and Critical Aspects of a Development Program," *Fund Raising Management* 27, no. 5 (July 1996): 36-39.

Hartsook, Robert F. "But Have You Really Said Thank You?: Good Stewardship Is Not Just Sending a Receipt for a Gift. Think of Unique Ways to Say Thank You to Donors," *Fund Raising Management* 26, no. 1 (March 1995): 42-

King, Heather. "The Power of the Challenge: A Small Shop Uses a Challenge Grant to Achieve Big Results," CURRENTS 25, no. 6 (June 1999): 15.

King, R. King, and Chuck Crowe. "A Unique Alumni Challenge: Central Wesleyan College Not Only Won $50,000 for its First-Place Finish in the Alumni Challenge, but it Also Rekindled Alumni Giving," *Fund Raising Management* 4, no. 6 (August 1993): 23-

Kirkman, Kay. "Thanks Again—And Again: Seven Simple Steps to a Successful Donor Recognition Program," CURRENTS 21, no. 8 (September 1995): 38-40.

Kirkman, Kay. "To Fund the Impossible Dream: Iowa State University Created a Plaza of Heroines with Paving Bricks to Honor Women. The Goal: Raise $200,000 to Honor 2,000 Women. The Campaign Raised $400,000 and Honored 3,000 Women," *Fund Raising Management* 26, no. 6 (August 1995): 2-23.

Logan, Frank A. "Starting a Donor Recognition Society," *Give and Take* 27, no. 4 (April 1995): 5-6.

Martin, Gary J. "Thanks in Advance: How Recognizing Planned Gifts Can Help Get More and Bigger Donations," CURRENTS 16, no. 5 (May 1990): 22-26.

McNay, Linda Wise. "Rising to the Challenge: Making the Most of Gifts that Leverage Gifts," CURRENTS 18, no. 4 (April 1992): 18-22.

Peirce, Susan P. *Gift Club Programs: A Survey of How 44 Institutions Raise Money.* Washington, DC: Council for Advancement and Support of Education, 1992. 60 pages.

Phair, Judith T. "Rethinking Annual Reports: A New Look at the Old Standby of the Campus Publications Office," CURRENTS 18, no. 3 (March 1992): 44-48, 51.

Philanthropic Services for Institutions. *Accent on Recognition: Saying Thank You to Donors and Volunteers.* Philanthropic Services for Institutions, 1991. 100 pages.

Pollack, Rachel H. "Thanks for the Memories: A Dozen One-of-a-Kind Ways Institutions Reflect Campus Traditions When Recognizing Donors," CURRENTS 24, no. 8 (September 1998): 24-28, 30-31.

Ruda, Tammie L. "Up Where They Belong: Done Right, Gift Clubs Can Raise Donors' Sights and Create a Sense of Community. Here's How to Create Prestigious Clubs that Meet Your Goals," CURRENTS 25, no. 1 (January 1999): 40-46.

Ryan, Ellen. "Many Means of Thanks: Donor Recognition Doesn't Have to Be Expensive—But it Must Be Personal and Sincere. Five Examples Tell the Tale," CURRENTS 21, no. 8 (September 1995): 41-42.

Ryan, J. Patrick. "Thanks a Million: You Need Strong Recognition Programs to Foster Healthy Donor Relations," CURRENTS 20, no. 3 (March 1994): 64.

Shubeck, Theresa. "For Donors Who Have Everything: Major Givers Hardly Need Another Bronze Plaque. Here's How to Say Thank You with Sincerity and Creativity," CURRENTS 16, no. 10 (November/December 1990): 52-57.

Taylor, John H. "The Morning After: You Finally Got that Big Gift. Here's What to Do Next," CURRENTS 22, no. 10 (November/December 1996): 30-32.

"Thanking Matching Gift Companies: Survey of Top Companies Identifies Acknowledgment and Recognition Preferences," *Matching Gift Notes* 9, no. 1 (Fall 1991): 2-3.

Watts, Susan. "Recognizing Your Forgotten Donors," *Fund Raising Management* 28, no. 4 (June 1997): 32-33.

Wolfe, Audley (Buddy) Jr. "Volunteer Phone Thank-a-Thons: Minimal Investment-High Returns: Calling Donors Just to Say Thanks Not Only Surprises Them, but Opens the Door to Bigger Gifts, More Accurate Records and Deeper Donor Involvement," *Fund Raising Management* 24, no. 1 (March 1993): 43-

ANNUAL GIVING: MARKETING AND MARKET RESEARCH SEGMENTATION

Absher, Keith, and Gerald Crawford. "Marketing the Community College Starts with Understanding Students' Perspectives," *Community College Review* 23, no. 4 (Spring 1996): 59-68.

Ahles, Catherine B. "Red-Hot Research: New and Improved Market Research Technologies Are Heating Up on Campus. Here's How You Can Use Them to Reach Your Key Audiences—and Keep Their Attention," CURRENTS 24, no. 9 (October 1998): 24-29.

Arbeiter, Larry. "Save the News Bureaus! Integrated Marketing May Be All the Rage, but it's Not the Solution for Everyone. Here's Why," CURRENTS 24, no. 1 (January 1998): 30-31.

Authers, John. "The Student as Customer: Marketing Strategies of UK Further Education Colleges," *Financial Times,* no. 32780 (September 14, 1995): 21.

Benson, Mary Ellen. "A Jury of Their Peers: Let Focus Groups of High School Students Be the True Judge of Your Recruitment Publications," CURRENTS 25, no. 2 (February 1999): 44-49.

Cleary, Sean. "A New Order of Things: The University of Michigan Alumni Association Reinvents Itself as a Market-Focused Organization," CURRENTS 25, no. 6 (June 1999): 38-43.

Cornforth, Suzanne R., and William Koty. "Untangling the Web: It Takes More than Counting Hits to Evaluate Your Web Site's Success—Or Troubles. Here's How to Find Out Who Your Visitors Are, What They Want, and How They Want It," CURRENTS 23, no. 7 (July/August 1997): 10-16.

Dorsey, Cathryn Seymour. *Classic Currents: Market Research: Planning; Survey Design; Mail, Telephone, and Readership Surveys; Turning Results into Programs and More.* Edited by Cathryn Seymour Dorsey. Washington, DC: Council for Advancement and Support of Education, May 1998. 32 pages.

Ferrari, Michael R., and Larry D. Lauer. "Vision of the Future: Move Integrated Marketing Out of the Communications Office and into the Entire Institution with Participatory Strategic Planning," CURRENTS 26, no. 4 (April 2000): 18-22.

Herron, Douglas B. *Marketing Nonprofit Programs and Services: Proven and Practical Strategies to Get More Customers, Members and Donors.* San Francisco, CA: Jossey-Bass Publishers, 1996. 302 pages.

Kitchen, Philip. *Marketing Communications: Principles and Practice.* London, England: International Thomson Business Press, 1999.

Kotler, Philip, and Karen F.A. Fox. *Strategic Marketing for Educational Institutions.* 2nd ed. Englewood Cliffs, NJ: Prentice Hall Publishers, 1995. 484 pages.

Lauer, Larry D. "Marketing Across the Board: Have You Got What it Takes to Launch an Integrated Marketing Program? Follow These Eight Steps for a Successful Takeoff," CURRENTS 25, no. 1 (January 1999): 18-24.

Lauer, Larry D. "Need Visibility? Get Integrated: Campus Communicators Are Natural Leaders for Integrated Marketing Programs. Here's Why—And How to Pull it Off," CURRENTS 24, no. 1 (January 1998): 12-19.

Lawlor, John. "Brand Identity: Is Your Campus Getting Lost in the Crowd? To Stand Out, Try a Corporate Technique Called Branding," CURRENTS 24, no. 9 (October 1998): 16-23.

Martin, Patricia. "In the Company of Sponsors: With the Recent Growth in Corporate Sponsorship of Not-for-Profits, Organizations Cannot Afford to Ignore Their Revenue-Generating Potential. Gaining a Commercial Partner Requires Some Marketing Savvy and a Strong Sense of Organizational Identity," *Advancing Philanthropy* 4, no. 1 (Spring 1996): 30-35.

McNamee, Thomas. "The Power of Story: How Listening to Your Graduates Draws Them Closer to Alma Mater—And Brings Out Their Desire to Give," CURRENTS 20, no. 7 (July/August 1994): 28-32.

Moore, Robert M. "Putting More into Marketing: Highlights from Lipman Hearne's Second Integrated Marketing Survey," CURRENTS 26, no. 4 (April 2000): 38-41.

Moore, Robert M. "Surveying the Field: A 1998 Study Reveals the Strengths and Weaknesses of Campus Integrated Marketing Efforts," CURRENTS 25, no. 1 (January 1999): 26-29.

Plank, Richard. "A 'Brand' New Perspective: Using a Campaign to Promote an Institution's Brand," CURRENTS 26, no. 4 (April 2000): 13-14.

Pollack, Rachel H. "Signs Point to Yes: To Develop More Effective Appeals, Stanford's Jerold Pearson Applies the Science of Market Research to the Art of Advancement," CURRENTS 26, no. 4 (April 2000): 32-37.

"Relationship Marketing: A New Marketing Concept for Higher Education," *Marketing Higher Education* 10, no. 4 (April 1996): 1-5.

Sevier, Robert. "Research: The First Frontier: Integrated Marketing Programs Are Based on Knowledge of Your Audience. Use This Market Research Guide to Get It," CURRENTS 24, no. 1 (January 1998): 20-24.

Sevier, Robert A. "Image is Everything—Strategies for Measuring, Changing, and Maintaining Your Institution's Image," *College and University* 69, no. 2 (Winter 1994): 60-75.

Sevier, Robert A. *Integrated Marketing for Colleges, Universities, and Schools: A Step by Step Planning Guide.* Washington, DC: Council for Advancement and Support of Education, 1999. 218 pages.

Sevier, Robert A., and Robert E. Johnson. *Integrated Marketing Communication: A Practical Guide to Developing Comprehensive Communication Strategies.* Editor. Washington, DC: Council for Advancement and Support of Education, 1999. 300 pages.

Topor, Bob. "Don't Underestimate the Value of Your Parent Institution's Image," *Marketing Higher Education* 10, no. 2 (February 1996): 1-2.

VandenBerg, Patricia R. "Singular Sensation: Developing and Rolling Out a Unified Brand Identity for the University of Massachusetts," CURRENTS 26, no. 4 (April 2000): 24-30.

Weinstein, Art. *Market Segmentation: Using Demographics, Psychographics, and Other Niche Marketing Techniques to Predict and Model Customer Behavior*. Revised Edition. Burr Ridge, IL: Irwin Professional Publishing, 1994. 313 pages.

ANNUAL GIVING: PHONATHONS—TIPS AND TECHNIQUES

Carney, Joe. "Defending Our Honor: We Need to Convince Our Alumni that Student Callers Aren't Telemarketers. The Difference? Students Care About Our Cause," CURRENTS 20, no. 8 (September 1994): 64.

Carter, Lindy Keane. *Classic Currents: Annual Giving: 14 Articles on Planning, Mail and Phone Solicitations, Closing the Year Successfully, Tips from the Experts, and More*. Compiled by Lindy Keane Carter. Washington, DC: Council for Advancement and Support of Education, 1998.

"Dealing with Objections: For Every Reason Not to Give, There's a More Compelling Reason to Give. Here's How to Turn Common Donor Objections into Stronger Cases for Support," CURRENTS 23, no. 4 (April 1997): 28-33.

Dunn, Stephen. "Telemarketing in the 90s: Rising Above the Plateau: A Telemarketer Offers 10 Points to Examine in an Effort to Jump-Start a Stalled Campaign. Almost Every Telemarketing Campaign Can Improve its Results with One or More of These Points," *Fund Raising Management* 26, no. 2 (April 1995): 25-27.

Hazen, Harold P. "Oh No! Not Another Telemarketing Call! Telemarketing Is Not for Everybody. But if You Need to Reach a Large Audience Quickly in Order to Expand Your Base, Identify Leads, Qualify

Prospects and Add Donors, Telemarketing Might Do the Trick," *Fund Raising Management* 27, no. 1 (March 1996): 35-37.

Heuermann, Robert. "A Higher Calling: Your Fund-Raising Efforts Are Crucial to the Future. Here's Why," CURRENTS 23, no. 4 (April 1997): 16-18.

Kalafut-Wronko, Deborah. "How to Choose a Telemarketing Firm for Fund Raising: Choose a Telemarketing Firm Carefully. It Has the Power to Not Only Make or Break a Campaign, but More Importantly it Can Make or Break the Reputation of Your Organization," *Fund Raising Management* 27, no. 1 (March 1996): 20-22.

Kinney, Mark, and Ellen Goerlich. "University Builds Successful Phonathon: By Developing a System Model, an Organization Can Not Only Create a Strategic Plan, but also Have an Ongoing Evaluation Process that Will Focus Attention on Elements that Impact Campaign Results the Most," *Fund Raising Management* 27, no. 1 (March 1996): 28-33.

Logan, Timothy D. "Managing the Telemarketing Process: Forecasting Fund-Raising Income: Accurately Forecasting Telemarketing Income Helps Fund Raisers to Educate Board Members About the Telemarketing Process," *Fund Raising Management* 26, no. 2 (April 1995): 30-33.

"Making the Call: A Step-by-Step Guide from "Hello" to "Thank You, Goodbye"—And Everything in Between," CURRENTS 23, no. 4 (April 1997): 24-27.

McBrearty, Bruce, and Marcia C. Calhoun. "Reinventing Telephone Marketing: Those Who Accept the Challenge of Taking Telephone Marketing to the Next Level Through Scripting, Direct Mail and More Narrow File Selection Will Enjoy the Medium's Full Benefits," *Fund Raising Management* 25, no. 2 (April 1994): 54-

McNamee, Mike. "Dealing with Donor Anger: Sure, the Public Is Mad About Junk Mail and Junk Calls. But Campus Fund Raisers Don't Have to Worry About Hostile Alumni—Or Do They?," CURRENTS 21, no. 4 (April 1995): 16-21.

Metz, Amy Talbert. "Welcome to Camp Phonathon: Here's How to Transform Your Callers from Raw Recruits into Polished Campus Ambassadors," CURRENTS 23, no. 4 (April 1997): 10-14.

"Phonathon Phollies: You'll Laugh, You'll Cry, You'll Motivate Your Callers by Relating These True Tales from the Trenches," CURRENTS 23, no. 4 (April 1997): 64.

Pollack, Rachel H. "Hold the Phone: Use Higher Asks, Better Fulfillment, and Motivated Callers to Bring in More Telemarking Dollars," CURRENTS 24, no. 5 (May 1998): 28-32.

"Post-Flood Phonathons...And Other Ways to Meet a Crisis Fund-Raising Need," CURRENTS 23, no. 7 (July/August 1997): 8-9.

Ryan, Ellen. "Annual Fund Answers: Experts in Direct Mail, Phonathons, and In-Person Asks Tackle Some of the Annual Fund's Perennial Problems," CURRENTS 22, no. 5 (May 1996): 30-

Taylor, Amy Jo. "Big Things from Small Packages: How to Motivate Student Callers in Tight Places on a Tight Budget," CURRENTS 24, no. 5 (May 1998): 64.

"Tips for Calling Success: These Do's and Don'ts Will Keep Your Calls Running Smoothly," CURRENTS 23, no. 4 (April 1997): 20-23.

Twardowski, Timothy. "The Future of Telephone Fund Raising: Over the Next Decade Non-Profits Will Face Challenges Ranging from Increased Government Regulation to Harnessing the Awesome Potential of Expanding Communications Technology," *Fund Raising Management* 25, no. 1 (March 1994): 43-

Wallace, Jodi M. "Universities Graduate to Call Center Automation," *Fund Raising Management* 27, no. 9 (November 1996): 26-29.

Warwick, Mal. "Telephone Tactics: Seven Steps to Make Your Phonathon Script a Winner from 'Hello' to 'Thank You and Good Night'," CURRENTS 22, no. 5 (May 1996): 24-

ANNUAL GIVING: REUNION FUND RAISING

Lange, Scott R., and Ellen Ryan. "Thanks for the Memories: Start a Reunion Gift Program to Help Returning Alumni Help Your Institution," CURRENTS 16, no. 9 (October 1990): 14-19.

McHugh, G. Michael. "More than a Sentimental Journey: Give Your Alumni Something to Think About with a Reunion Mini-College," CURRENTS 10, no. 2 (February 1984): 26-27.

Nicklin, Julie L. "Tapping the Reunion: Fund Raisers for John Carroll U. Show How the Annual Alumni Event Can Pay Off," *Chronicle of Higher Education* 40, no. 44 (July 6, 1994): A25, A28.

Pollack, Rachel H. "Divide and Conquer: Get More from Your Annual Fund by Targeting Appeals to Special Groups," CURRENTS 24, no. 5 (May 1998): 12-19.

Willemain, Thomas R. "Alumni Giving: The Influences of Reunion, Class, and Year," *Research in Higher Education* 35, no. 5 (October 1994): 609-629.

ANNUAL GIVING: THE ANNUAL FUND AND THE CAMPAIGN

Anderson, Christian. "Cash on the Barrelhead: How Campuses Are Making the Active Case for Endowment Funds Now," CURRENTS 18, no. 10 (November/December 1992): 26-28, 30, 32.

"Expert Advice: Consultants Tell How to Handle Several Campaign Conundrums," CURRENTS 21, no. 10 (November/December 1995): 72-

Gafke, Roger. "Carving a Piece of the Action for the Annual Fund: So Your Organization Is Heading for a Capital Campaign in the Next Year or So? You're the Annual Fund Director. You Worry that Your Budget-Pocket Will Be Picked by Those Planning the Major Gift Effort, Your Annual Goals Will Remain High, Your Best Prospects Will Be Off-Limits, and the Recognition for Those Who Do Support the Annual Giving Program Will Be Minuscule Compared to that Accorded Campaign Contributors," *Advancing Philanthropy* 6, no. 2 (Summer 1998): 22-23.

Gearhart, G. David. *The Capital Campaign in Higher Education: A Practical Guide for College and University Advancement.* Washington, DC: National Association of College and University Business Officers, 1995. 222 pages.

Goodale, Toni K. "Consultant's Corner: Maintaining the Annual Fund," *Fund Raising Management* 27, no. 1 (March 1996): 54-55.

Kling, Paul F. "Planned Giving and Annual Giving Can Cooperate: Planned Giving and Annual Giving Are an Uneasy Fit, but the Payoff for Working Together Can Be Enormous," *Fund Raising Management* 23, no. 12 (February 1993): 53-

Koelzer, Joyce D. "Matchmaker, Matchmaker: Twenty-Three Ideas for Encouraging Corporate Matching Gifts from Your Annual Fund Donors," CURRENTS 18, no. 2 (February 1992): 6-10.

Lane, Margaret M. "The Role of the Annual Fund in a Capital Campaign," Master's thesis, DePaul University, 1992.

O'Shea, Catherine L. "Fasten Your Seatbelts: When Your Campaign Encounters Turbulence, Try These Tips for Riding Out the Bumps," CURRENTS 26, no. 1 (January 2000): 13.

Rechseen, Donna M., and Thomas R. Poole. "The Anatomy of an Endowment/Capital Campaign: The Right Campaign Leadership Can Overcome the Most Difficult Set of Circumstances—Even War, Recession and Unprecedented Change in the Health-Care Field. Long Beach Memorial Medical Center Is a Case in Point," *Fund Raising Management* 27, no. 6 (August 1996): 14-18.

Rillera-Martinez, Lyric A. "Small-Scale Winnings: Guiding a Motivated Group of Donors on a Special Project Is a Gamble that Can Pay Off," CURRENTS 17, no. 5 (May 1991): 46-47.

Sabo, Sandra R. "Double Duty: How Should You Handle Your Annual Fund During a Capital Campaign? Don't Let the Annual Fund Wither from Neglect," CURRENTS 21, no. 10 (November/December 1995): 26-

Wildern, William J. "Planned Giving: Keeping the Balance: Planned Giving Is Only Part of a Well-Rounded Fund-Raising Program Consisting of Capital Campaigns, Major Gifts, Annual Funds and Special Events. It's a Question of Balance," *Fund Raising Management* 21, no. 12 (February 1991): 50, 52-53.

ANNUAL GIVING: VOLUNTEER RECRUITMENT, MANAGEMENT, AND MOTIVATION

Anderson, L. McTier. "Managing Volunteers: The Effective Management of Volunteers Can Ensure Success for a Non-Profit and Bring Great Satisfaction to the Volunteers Themselves," *Fund Raising Management* 23, no. 6 (August 1992): 43-

Borenstein, Henry P. "Resources Unused Are Resources Abused Syndrome: Board Members Are Chosen for Their Contacts and Resources. Some Fail to Accept This Responsibility. This Problem Must Be Dealt with Sensitively but Decisively Before It Infects the Entire Board," *Fund Raising Management* 27, no. 6 (August 1996): 20-23.

Brody, Leslie. *Effective Fund Raising Tools and Techniques for Success.* Acton, MA: Copley Publishing Group, 1994. 157 pages.

Cantore, Jean Ann. "Putting It All Together: How Fund Raiser and Researcher Can Cooperate to Make Every Solicitation More than the Sum of its Parts," CURRENTS 22, no. 10 (November/December 1996): 12-16.

Carter, Lindy Keane, and Stewart Saltonstall. "Group Dynamics: Despite Their Differences, Your Development Committee Volunteers Can Work as a Team for Solid Fund-Raising Results," CURRENTS 24, no. 1 (January 1998): 34-39.

Connors, Tracy Daniel. *The Volunteer Management Handbook.* New York, NY: John Wiley and Sons Inc., 1995. 407 pages.

"A Couple of Campaign Chairs: Husband and Wife Volunteers Share What They've Learned About Wealth, Women, and Working as a Team," CURRENTS 22, no. 8 (September 1996): 9.

Dean, James. "Leadership: The Engine of Development: Development Staff Performs Best When it Drives the Campaign from the Rear. Let the Volunteers Stay in Front and Lead," *Fund Raising Management* 26, no. 1 (March 1995): 14-

Evans, Gary. *Development Committee.* Washington, DC: Association of Governing Boards of Universities and Colleges, 1996. 12 pages.

George, G. Worth. "Releasing Your Board's Potential: The Vexing Problem of Boards and Fund Raising Is in Reality One of Identification and Recruitment of Persons of Influence with Potential for Growth, Even if Not Possessed of Abundant Means," *Fund Raising Management* 26, no. 8 (October 1995): 50-54.

Goodale, Toni. "Use Them or Lose Them: How to Identify, Recruit and Motivate Volunteers," *Fund Raising Management* 25, no. 12 (February 1995): 48-49.

Greenfield, James M. *Fund Raising Fundamentals: A Guide to Annual Giving for Professionals and Volunteers.* New York, NY: John Wiley and Sons Inc., 1994. 407 pages.

Grimes, Gail Terry. "Volunteers: Stars of Every Special Event: With Fund-Raising Professionals Concentrating on Soliciting Major Gifts, the Future of Special Events Rests with Volunteers. They Can Give the Time the Staff Cannot Spare," *Fund Raising Management* 25, no. 8 (October 1994): 12-

Hicks, John W. "When Your Volunteer Is a High Mucketymuck: They Have Power, Prestige, Assets and Access. They Also Have Egos, Fears, Limitations and Hesitations. To Make Use of Executive Volunteers' Strengths, You Need to Know How to Get Around Their Weaknesses," *Advancing Philanthropy* 4, no. 2 (Summer 1996): 36-37.

Howe, Fisher. *The Board Members' Guide to Fund Raising: What Every Trustee Needs to Know About Raising Money.* Washington, DC: Jossey-Bass Publishers and the National Center for Nonprofit Boards, 1991. 140 pages.

Jones, Jeremy. "Askophobia: Most of Your Volunteers Feel Uncomfortable Asking for Money. This Training Technique Will Help Overcome Their Fears," CURRENTS 19, no. 10 (November/December 1991): 22-29.

Joyaux, Simone P. *Strategic Fund Development: Building Profitable Relationships that Last.* Frederick, MD: Aspen Publishers, March 1997. 213 pages.

Lowery, William R. "Divide and Conquer: Pairing the Right Trustee with the Right Task Will Make Board Members a More Effective Part of Your Development Team," CURRENTS 19, no. 8 (September 1993): 41-42, 44, 46.

Maude, Michael, and Richard Heap. "Catapult Your Development Efforts with an Advisory Council," *Fund Raising Management* 28, no. 3 (May 1997): 24-29.

McGannon, J. Barry. "Who Should Ask for the Gift?: The Staff," CURRENTS 18, no. 1 (January 1992): 14-16, 18.

Miller, Barbara. "Creative Brainstorming with Your Board," *Fund Raising Management* 27, no. 11 (January 1997): 18-20.

Nelson, Dave. "Do We Need Volunteers in Special Events?" *Fund Raising Management* 29, no. 2 (April 1998): 19, 48.

Outhouse, William L. "Do the Right Things: Four Success Strategies for Small Shops on a Shoestring," CURRENTS 17, no. 9 (October 1991): 42-44.

Ryan, Ellen. "On the Phone Again: Sixty Ways to Train Your Callers, Motivate Your Donors, and Maintain Your Sanity," CURRENTS 17, no. 3 (March 1991): 28-32.

Ryan, John S. "Volunteers Can Run an Endowment Program," *Fund Raising Management* 24, no. 12 (February 1994): 39-

Sherbondy, Robert E. "The Effective Enlistment of Volunteers: In Any Fund-Raising Campaign, People in the Right Position Are Crucial to the Success of the Overall Effort," *Fund Raising Management* 23, no. 6 (August 1992): 28-

Williams, B. Jeanne. "What Volunteers Can Expect from You, and Vice Versa: They Come to You with the Best of Intentions. They Want to Give of Themselves, to Do Meaningful Work, to Make a Difference. You Need to Spell Out Their Rights (and Your Own) if You Want Them to Stay Around and Succeed," *Advancing Philanthropy* 4, no. 2 (Summer 1996): 34-35.

Woolbright, Cynthia, and Heather Calvin. "The Strategic Annual Fund: How Smith College Overhauled its Efforts, Assumptions, and Goals—And Set Fund-Raising Success in Motion," CURRENTS 22, no. 8 (September 1996): 45-49.

ANNUAL GIVING: YOUNG ALUMNI AND SENIOR CLASS GIFTS

Adams, Rick. "Lifestyles of the Young and Driven: Even a Well-Established Association Can Get Behind the Times. Here's How One College Grapples with Today's Alumni," CURRENTS 18, no. 8 (September 1992): 28-32, 34.

Conklin, Linda. "Help Wanted: More than Anything Else, Young Alumni Are Seeking Career Advice. Show You're Qualified to Meet Their Needs by Offering These Four Services," CURRENTS 24, no. 6 (June 1998): 22-23.

Dessoff, Alan L. "Programming Partners: Need Lessons on How to Co-Sponsor Student Programs? Here's Some Fancy Footwork Your Alumni Office Can Use," CURRENTS 20, no. 9 (October 1994): 26-30.

Espeseth, Terry Dennison. "Putting Your Best Foot Forward: Eight Steps to Promote Your Alumni Office and Create Lasting Campus Ties," CURRENTS 20, no. 9 (October 1994): 28.

Henderson, Nancy. "New Gifts from New Graduates: Instill the Giving Habit Early with These Techniques to Encourage Involvement from Young Alumni," CURRENTS 23, no. 1 (January 1997): 42-46.

Hunter, Barbara Martin. "Fun for All Ages: Want to Plan a Reunion with Mass Appeal? These Ideas Can Help You Draw Everyone from Babies to Baby Boomers, Young Alumni to Older Graduates," CURRENTS 22, no. 9 (October 1996): 14-18.

Jackson, Laura Christion. "Inside Information: What Do Your Young Alumni Want? Recent Graduates Involved with the Alumni Profession Reveal Five Strategies You Can Use to Improve Services," CURRENTS 24, no. 6 (June 1998): 18.

Jackson, Laura Christion. "Keeping Up with the Crowd: Trying to Connect with Your Recent Graduates? Consider this Sampling of Successful Ideas for Finding, Involving, and Motivating New Alumni," CURRENTS 24, no. 6 (June 1998): 20-24.

Jackson, Laura Christion. "On the Road to Alumni: If You Want Involved Graduates Tomorrow, Steer Your Students in the Right Direction Today. This Year-by-Year Road Map Can Help," CURRENTS 20, no. 9 (October 1994): 20-24.

Kennedy, Marilyn Moats. "X Marks the Spot: Ideas for Targeting Your Alumni Association to Career-Driven, Cash-Strapped Recent Graduates," CURRENTS 24, no. 6 (June 1998): 16-19.

McDaniel, Sheila A. "Joint Ventures in Volunteering: Community Service Projects Can Bring Current and Former Students Closer to Campus—and Each Other," CURRENTS 20, no. 3 (March 1994): 52.

Nuza, Jessica. "A Powerful Network: Student Advancement Programs Are Another Valuable Way to Prepare Your Future Alumni. Here's How They Made a Difference in 1997-98," CURRENTS 24, no. 6 (June 1998): 12-13.

Pollack, Rachel H. "Divide and Conquer: Get More from Your Annual Fund by Targeting Appeals to Special Groups," CURRENTS 24, no. 5 (May 1998): 12-19.

Schoultz, Cathleen O'Conner. "Getting the Busters and Keeping the Boomers: Mission Impossible? Nah. But if You're Clueless About How to Accomplish a Harmonious Buster-Boomer Membership Blend for Your Association, Here's Help," *Association Management* 49, no. 6 (June 1997): 44, 47-49.

Todd, Jeffrey S. "Something for Everyone: Young Alumni Can Also Benefit from Continuing Education—If You Use Creative Ways to Catch Their Interest," CURRENTS 20, no. 2 (February 1994): 28-32.

Toward, Christopher. "The Young and the Restless: Alumni in Their 20s, 30s, and 40s Can Be an Untapped Source of Major Gifts for Your Campus, but They May Not Sit Still for the Usual Appeals," CURRENTS 25, no. 2 (February 1999): 26-31.

Vassallo, Philip. "Playing Their Song: Is Your Alumni Office Out of Tune with Today's Students? Here's How to Get Them on Your Hit Parate Before Commencement," CURRENTS 24, no. 6 (June 1998): 10-15.

This bibliography was prepared by the Information Center at the Council for Advancement and Support of Education (CASE).

* When ordering publications from CASE Books, VISA, Mastercard, American Express, checks, money orders, and purchase order forms are accepted. Prepayment in U.S. dollars required. There are additional charges for shipping and handling, foreign orders, and rush service. Please include the product title and item number when calling. CASE Books, Dept. 4022, Washington, DC 20042-4022. Phone: (800) 554-8536 or (301) 604-2068. Fax: (301) 206-9789. Also visit www.case.org/books to see the CASE Books online catalog.